THREE PLAYS FOR CHILDREN

Phil Clark trained as an Actor/Teacher at Rose Bruford College of Speech and Drama, London, and Durham University, and has a PhD from the University of Glamorgan, Wales. He has directed plays for companies all over Britain, and was Artistic Director of the Sherman Theatre, Cardiff, where he commissioned more than 120 new plays for young audiences. He was previously Artistic Director of the Crucible Theatre In Education and Community Company in Sheffield, and won the British Theatre Association Drama Review Award. In 1994 he won the Canadian Institute Arts for Young Audiences Award. He teaches at a number of theatre schools and works regularly with the National Association of Youth Theatre. He continues to specialise in theatre for young audiences.

Oscar Wilde

THREE PLAYS FOR CHILDREN

THE DEVOTED FRIEND

THE HAPPY PRINCE

THE SELFISH GIANT

Adapted for the stage
By Phil Clark

OBERON BOOKS
LONDON

First published in 2007 by Oberon Books Ltd
Electronic edition published in 2012

Oberon Books Ltd
521 Caledonian Road, London N7 9RH
Tel: 020 7607 3637 / Fax: 020 7607 3629
e-mail: info@oberonbooks.com
www.oberonbooks.com

A catalogue record for this book is available from the British Library.

PB ISBN: 978-1-84002-816-4
Digital ISBN: 978-1-84943-346-4

Cover illustration by John Angus

Visit www.oberonbooks.com to read more about all our books and to buy them. You will also find features, author interviews and news of any author events, and you can sign up for e-newsletters so that you're always first to hear about our new releases.

Contents

Introduction

ALTHOUGH Oscar Wilde's stories for young people were written over a hundred years ago, they still retain an immense contemporary relevance. Wilde was a great storyteller, and it is said that he wrote these stories for his own children. Often they have simple narratives with strong emotional, dramatic and complex relationships. He recognised that young people are complex human beings, and his exploration of themes such as happiness, devotion, bullying, friendship and selfishness demand that the reader responds with intensive thought.

The plays in this volume were originally commissioned and performed by the Sherman Theatre Company in Cardiff for young people between the ages of 3 and 8. The company performed them at the Sherman theatre itself and toured them to community centres, arts centres, theatres and schools throughout Wales. Although written for professional actors, they are extremely performable by youth theatres and drama clubs and schools. Each of the plays can be performed by three actors, but should a group choose to, there is no reason why more actors couldn't be used. They demand strong artistic invention from the company. The scripts can also be used as classroom readers, and many of the themes in the stories have direct relevance to the national teaching curriculum.

Adapting *The Selfish Giant*, *The Happy Prince* and *The Devoted Friend* for the stage was a great challenge. There is no doubt that young people adore Wilde's stories, and the adaptations are intended to remain faithful to them. Essentially, these three plays ask the audience to care about the characters on stage. Together, they present a new opportunity to introduce young people to the stories of one of Britain's greatest writers.

Phil Clark, 2007

THE DEVOTED FRIEND

Characters

Actor 1 GARETH
LITTLE HANS

Actor 2 NICK
HUGH THE MILLER

Actor 3 LLINOS
NARRATOR
HUGH'S WIFE
A NEIGHBOUR
THE DOCTOR

A puppet dressed in the same costume as Little Hans could be used when he goes on journeys and when he falls to his death.

The Devoted Friend was first performed by Sherman Cymru on 2 November 2007 with the following company:

ACTOR 1, Gareth Wyn Griffiths
ACTOR 2, Nick Wayland Evans
ACTOR 3, Llinos Mai

Director Phil Clark
Designer Tina Reeves
Lighting Designer Ceri James
Composer / Musical Director Lucy Rivers
Stage Managers Brenda Knight & Lorna Warrington

The audience sit around a large triangular performance space.
In each of the three corners is a large cupboard.
LLINOS enters the performance space.
She is wearing a storytelling cloak, which has motifs all over it from
stories. She sings:

LLINOS Telling stories
Telling stories
My imagination never fails

There are…
Kings and queens and princes galore
Lords and Ladies, rich and poor
Lions and tigers, killer sharks too
All caught up in a story for you

Telling stories
Telling stories
My imagination never fails

During the song she ties a label on each of the cupboard
doors.
Cupboard 1 has a label on it that reads 'For Gareth'.
It is full of materials, silks, quilts, etc, everything
he will need to create a garden environment. The
cupboard will become his house.
Cupboard 2 has a label on it that reads 'For Nick'. It
is full of musical instruments and everything needed
to make the music and sound for the show.
Cupboard 3 has a label on it that reads 'For Llinos'. It
is full of dressing-up clothes that include the costumes
for the characters in the story.
At the end of the song she takes off the storytelling
cloak and puts it into Cupboard 3.
She hides.

GARETH enters the space.
He looks around.

He hums to himself.
He goes up to Cupboard 3 and reads the label.

GARETH 'For Nick'
     That's not me

He goes up to Cupboard 2 and reads the label.

'For Llinos'
That's not me

He goes up to Cupboard 1 and reads the label.

'For Gareth'
That's me

He carries on reading the label.

'This is all you need
Open me and play
P.S. don't forget to have fun'

He giggles.
He opens the cupboard and lots of material falls out, silks, quilts, etc, everything he needs to make a beautiful garden with the cupboard becoming his house. He plays with the material with great joy and excitement. This should be a celebration of play. It should be inventive and glorious with lots of laughter. Eventually after he has built his house and garden he settles down and gets comfortable and sleeps. He is content. He is hidden under the quilt.

NICK enters the scene.
He is thrilled by the garden environment.
He explores it.
Eventually he comes across Cupboard 3.
He reads the label.

NICK 'For Llinos'
   That's not me

He goes to Cupboard 2 and reads the label.

'For Nick'
That's me

Continues reading.

'Open me and listen to all the sounds
Play with them
P.S. don't forget to have fun'

He opens the cupboard.
It is full of musical instruments and sound makers.
He tries them out, blowing, strumming, shaking, etc.
He enjoys himself.
He makes one enormous sound and GARETH wakes
from under the quilt.

GARETH   What are you doing?

NICK   Playing

GARETH   Very noisy

NICK   Yes

GARETH   What are you playing?

NICK   Anything

GARETH   Anything?

NICK   Yes

GARETH   Can I play anything?

NICK   If you must. What were you doing?

GARETH   Sleeping

NICK   Sleeping?

GARETH   Yes

NICK   I haven't got time to sleep. I want to play. Is this
all your stuff?

GARETH   Yes. Well, it was in the cupboard with my name
                     on. Is that all your stuff?

NICK   Yes. It was in the cupboard with my name on.
                     What's that supposed to be?

GARETH   It's a garden. These are primroses, these are herbs.
                     These are my cherry trees and this is my house

NICK   I want to play in your garden

GARETH   Okay, you can make the sounds

*They begin to play together creating a beautiful garden.
They seem to be having fun, but NICK is definitely the
bossy one.*

GARETH brings out a box from inside his house.

NICK   What's in there?

GARETH   Things

NICK   What kind of things?

GARETH   Well, these are silver buttons for my best coat, this
                     is my best pipe and this is my very precious gold
                     chain

NICK   If you were my friend you would give them to me

GARETH   But they were in my cupboard

NICK   But friends should share things. I could let you
                     play my double bass. So I deserve your gold
                     chain

GARETH   But it is very precious to me

NICK   You just made that up

GARETH   Well, we're playing and that's what you do when
                     you play

NICK   What?

GARETH   Make things up. Pretend. It's fun

NICK   Yes, but I think you should give me your gold
          chain, like a good friend

LLINOS   Hi Gareth

GARETH   Hi Llinos

LLINOS   Hi Nick

NICK   Hi Llinos

LLINOS   What are you doing?

GARETH   Playing

NICK   Pretending

LLINOS   What are you playing?

NICK   Gareth's got a gold chain, but he won't give it to
          me

LLINOS   Whose is it?

NICK   Gareth's

GARETH   Well, it was in my cupboard

NICK   But he won't give it to me and I am his friend

LLINOS   What's in there?

          She indicates Cupboard 3.

NICK   Don't know

GARETH   Nor me

LLINOS   It's got my name on it

NICK   This one had my name on it

GARETH   And this one had my name on it

LLINOS   Well, this one must be mine then

NICK   Yes

GARETH   Cos you're Llinos

NICK   And I'm Nick

GARETH And I'm Gareth

LLINOS I'm going to open it

NICK I'll read the label for you

LLINOS I can do it myself thank you

NICK I'm just being friendly

LLINOS I know (*She reads.*)
'For Llinos
Open me
And be whoever you want to be
P.S. have fun'
I wonder what's inside

NICK Open it

LLINOS Shall I?

GARETH Yes, I'm really excited

NICK Please open it. I can't wait any longer

LLINOS I wonder what's inside

NICK Well, you'll never know unless you open it

LLINOS Here I go then

NICK At last

LLINOS opens the cupboard and lots of clothes fall out.

LLINOS Clothes

NICK Dressing-up clothes

LLINOS Yes, dressing-up clothes

GARETH Fantastic

LLINOS We could have great fun

NICK I'll get dressed up

LLINOS We could all dress up

NICK   And I could be important

LLINOS   You've got to guess who I am

NICK   Okay

She puts on a red cloak and hood.

LLINOS   Who am I?

The audience are encouraged to guess the character.

Yes, that's right, Little Red Riding Hood.

NICK   That was easy

LLINOS   Alright, try this one

She puts on a patchwork quilt and walks around as an elephant with a trunk.

NICK   I know, I know

GARETH   This one's harder

The audience shout out.

LLINOS   Yes, Elmer the Elephant

GARETH   More

NICK   Another one

She puts on a beautiful dress / ball gown and runs around and loses her shoe.

I know, I know

The audience shout out.

LLINOS   Yes, Cinderella

GARETH   This is great fun

NICK   I want a go. I want to pretend

LLINOS   I know, let's play, 'Let's Be'

ALL   (*Loudly.*) Yes, let's play 'Let's Be'

LLINOS   Let's be…

NICK   Kings

ALL   (*Loudly.*) Yes, let's be kings

They dress up and walk about pretending to be kings. GARETH holds up his gold chain.

GARETH   This is my royal chain

NICK   Let me wear it

GARETH   But

NICK   No, no, let's be gardeners

ALL   (*Loudly.*) Yes, let's be gardeners

They dress up as gardeners and walk about.

NICK   Plant the seeds

LLINOS   Pull up the weeds

GARETH   Water the flowers

NICK   And prune the trees

ALL   Plant the seeds
Pull up the weeds
Water the flowers
And trim the trees

This becomes the chorus to the Song of the Garden. They sing.

Plant the seeds
Pull up the weeds
Water the flowers
And trim the trees
Plant the seeds
Pull up the weeds
Water the flowers
And trim the trees

LLINOS   Will you help us with our song?

GARETH   You can pretend to be gardeners

NICK   Like us

SONG OF THE GARDEN

The characters teach the audience the actions to go with the chorus.

ALL   We have to…
(*Chorus.*) Plant the seeds
Pull up the weeds
Water the flowers
And trim the trees
Plant the seeds
Pull up the weeds
Water the flowers
And trim the trees

Our garden is so beautiful
It has lots of lovely flowers
With primroses and cherry trees
We work for hours and hours
We have to…
(*Chorus.*)

It changes in the springtime
Summer, autumn, winter too
It keeps us busy all year round
With lots of jobs to do
We have to…
(*Chorus.*)

LLINOS   That was great

GARETH   Well done everyone

LLINOS   I'm a great gardener

GARETH   So am I

NICK   I'm the best gardener in the world

LLINOS Now, where were we?

GARETH Let's be…

NICK Let's be…

LLINOS Best friends in our best clothes

ALL Yes, let's be best friends in our best clothes

LLINOS gives NICK and GARETH their costumes.
NICK puts on the costume of HUGH THE MILLER.
GARETH puts on the costume of LITTLE HANS.

GARETH Look at my coat
It's got silver buttons (*He attaches them.*)
It's my best coat

LLINOS You look fine in your best coat

NICK If you were my friend you would give me the coat

GARETH But it's my best one, and I am your friend

NICK Let me wear it then

LLINOS But it's Gareth's

NICK I thought you were my friend

GARETH I am

NICK I'll let you play my double bass

LLINOS Nick, why do you have to have everything that everybody else wants?

NICK Because we are friends and friends should be able to share everything

LLINOS But you always want what someone else has

NICK That's not true

LLINOS It is. You wanted Gareth's beautiful gold chain, and his best pipe and now you want his best coat with silver buttons

GARETH   He can have them, Llinos. I don't mind
He is my friend

LLINOS   That's very kind of you Gareth, but look what I've
got

She takes out her storytelling cloak from the cupboard.
It is beautiful and has lots of pictures and symbols on
it from stories.

GARETH   What is it?

LLINOS   It's my storytelling cloak

NICK   Can I have a go?

LLINOS   Just a minute

NICK   I'll let you play my double bass

GARETH   Tell us about your cloak, Llinos

LLINOS   Well

NICK   Come on

LLINOS   Well, you see all the pictures on the cloak

GARETH   Yes

LLINOS   I've got a story to go with every one of them

GARETH   Really?

LLINOS   Yes, look, here's Red Riding Hood, here's Elmer

GARETH   And there's Cinderella

NICK   What's that one?

He points at a picture of two hands in friendship.

LLINOS   Sometimes I make them up and sometimes they
are stories that everyone knows

GARETH   Sounds like great fun

LLINOS   It is

NICK   What's that one?

LLINOS I love telling tales

NICK You're not supposed to tell tales

LLINOS Not those sort of tales. I mean like fairy stories and tall stories.

(*Sings.*) There are...
Kings and queens and princes galore
Lords and ladies, rich and poor
Lions and tigers, killer sharks too
All caught up in a story for you

I'm always...
Telling stories
Telling tales
My imagination
Never fails

Could you help me with my song?

GARETH What do you want us to do?

LLINOS Put some music to it for me

NICK Oh, I suppose so

LLINOS Thank you both of you

Repeat the song with music.

GARETH I really enjoyed that

LLINOS Thank you Gareth

NICK What's that one?

LLINOS That's a very special one

NICK Why?

LLINOS Can you see the two hands?

GARETH Yes

LLINOS And they are hand in hand

NICK So?

LLINOS   Well, when do we see two hands hand in hand?

NICK   I know

GARETH   I know

LLINOS   Nick?

NICK   When you're arm wrestling

LLINOS   Gareth?

GARETH   When you're walking with your friend

LLINOS   Yes, hand in hand

NICK   Not always

LLINOS   But sometimes

NICK   But not always

LLINOS   Yes, Nick, but sometimes. Why do you have to be so difficult?

NICK   I'm not

LLINOS   Let me tell you both a story

NICK   Oh, I know lots of stories

LLINOS   I'm sure you do, but it was my idea first

GARETH   Tell us your story, Llinos

LLINOS   Well, I'm going to need your help, we can tell it together
Gareth?

GARETH   Yes, I'll help

LLINOS   Nick?

NICK   If I can tell a story next

LLINOS   Well, my story is about two friends and takes place in a garden and a flour mill

GARETH   This is my garden

LLINOS   Fantastic

SONG OF THE GARDEN

GARETH   My garden is so beautiful
         It has lots and lots of flowers
         With primroses and cherry trees
         I work for hours and hours

   ALL   Plant the seeds
         Pull up the weeds
         Water the flowers
         And trim the trees
         (*Repeat.*)

         By this point, all three cupboards look like they have
         exploded. Everything is now on stage to tell the story
         of The Devoted Friend.
         The stage is set.

LLINOS   And now for the people in my story.
         Once upon a time, there was an honest little
            fellow named Hans

  NICK   Is that me? Was he important? Was he grand?

LLINOS   No, it's you, Gareth. You can be Hans
         And no, he wasn't particularly important or grand
         But he had a very kind heart

  NICK   I could be Hans, I've got a kind heart

LLINOS   Just a minute, Nick, I've got another part for you.
         Now, where was I?

GARETH   Hans with the kind heart

LLINOS   Oh yes. He lived in a tiny cottage all by himself.
         He had a beautiful best coat with silver buttons.
         Put it on Gareth. A precious silver chain, a
         dusty old pipe, and a wheelbarrow. Every day

he worked in his beautiful garden. In all the
country there was no garden as lovely as his.

SONG OF THE GARDEN

GARETH   My garden is so beautiful
         It has lots and lots of flowers
         With primroses and cherry trees
         I work for hours and hours

         Plant the seeds
         Pull up the weeds
         Water the flowers
         And trim the trees

LLINOS   Little Hans had a great many friends, but his best
         friend was Hugh the Miller

NICK   Is that me?

LLINOS   Yes, that's you

NICK   Great. What's a miller?

LLINOS   Well when the farmer has cut the corn at the end
         of the summer they would take it to Hugh the
         Miller to be made into flour

NICK   How?

LLINOS   That's what the mill does

NICK   A mill?

LLINOS   Yes, that's where Hugh the Miller lived, in the
         Mill. The Mill crushed all the corn into flour
         for all the farmers to sell out at the market for
         people to make their bread

NICK   An important job then?

LLINOS   Yes, very important

NICK   And was he rich? Did he have lots of money?

LLINOS He did

GARETH Did Hans?

LLINOS No, he was poor

NICK But they were friends?

LLINOS Yes, great friends, best friends, devoted friends.
Hans lived in his cottage and Hugh lived in the
Mill

NICK And I'll build the Mill

*The story is now set up, and NICK and GARETH
become their characters. There is a change.*

SONG OF FRIENDSHIP

HANS Friend friend will you be my friend?
Friend friend will you be my friend?
Friend friend will you be my friend?

Friend friend will you be my friend?
In the coldest winter
Will you be my friend?
Should I fall or lose my way
Will you be my friend?
And if I have no food that day
Will you be my friend?

HUGH Hallo friend

HANS Hallo Friend

HUGH What a fine garden

HANS Why, thank you

HUGH Such beautiful flowers

HANS Aren't they?

HUGH   All the colours of the rainbow. I would love some
        flowers for my wife. May I just take these. Thank
        you dear friend

SONG OF FRIENDSHIP

BOTH   Friend friend will you be my friend?
        Friend friend will you be my friend?
        Friend friend will you be my friend?

HUGH   Hallo dear friend

HANS   Hallo best friend

HUGH   Your cherry trees are so full of fruit

HANS   Yes, it's a very good season for cherries

HUGH   Are they sweet and juicy?

HANS   They are indeed

HUGH   I must take some for my wife. Thank you dear
        friend for sharing your cherries with me

SONG OF FRIENDSHIP

BOTH   Friend friend will you be my friend?
        Friend friend will you be my friend?
        Friend friend will you be my friend?

NEIGHBOUR   Good morning Little Hans

HANS   Good morning Neighbour

NEIGHBOUR   What a glorious day

HANS   It is indeed

NEIGHBOUR   Your garden looks wonderful

HANS   Why thank you

NEIGHBOUR   And smells beautiful

HANS   Thank you again

NEIGHBOUR   Your flowers and herbs and cherry trees
            You must be very proud of it

HANS   I am indeed. I have very little in life but my
            garden. It is my pride and joy

NEIGHBOUR   You enjoy it dear friend

HANS   I will, I will. Would you like some nice ripe
            cherries?

NEIGHBOUR   That's very generous of you, but you keep them
            for yourself. Good day, and don't work too hard.

HANS   Good day

SONG OF FRIENDSHIP

HANS   Friend friend will you be my friend?
            Friend friend will you be my friend?
            Friend friend will you be my friend?

            Friend friend will you be my friend?
            On the hottest summer's day
            Will you be my friend?
            If I really need your help
            Will you be my friend?
            And if I've nothing left to share
            Will you be my friend?

            Friend friend will you be my friend?
            Friend friend will you be my friend?
            Friend friend will you be my friend?

LLINOS   Hans was always happy in spring, and the
            summer and the autumn. But in the winter when
            everything had died in the garden, Little Hans
            would stay indoors and try to keep warm. He
            often went to bed without any food.
            Hugh the Miller visited Hans in the spring and
            the summer and the autumn, but never in the

winter. He would stay at home in his warm Mill with his wife. She would often say:

WIFE Why don't you go and visit your friend Hans?

HUGH There is no good in my going to see my friend Hans in the middle of Winter

WIFE And why is that good husband?

HUGH Well, he is only happy when he is working in his garden and when the snow is on the ground he cannot work in his garden

WIFE But he still needs friends

HUGH I am sure he would not wish to see me when he is not happy and I am sure I am right

WIFE If you say so husband

HUGH I do indeed. I shall wait for the spring and then Little Hans will be able to give me a large basket of primroses and that will make him very happy

WIFE You are so thoughtful, so very thoughtful indeed. We could ask Little Hans to come and eat supper with us. If he is so sad in winter, I would happily give him a nice meal

HUGH But I am his friend, and I don't think that would be fair

WIFE I don't understand

HUGH Well, if Little Hans came here to our house and saw our lovely warm fire and delicious food and wine, I think that would be unfair

WIFE I don't understand

HUGH You see, good wife, Hans is a very good friend of mine. Indeed he is devoted to me. But he is very poor, and if he sees all our lovely things, he

might want them for himself. He might ask me
to lend him some flour for the winter

WIFE   And you could

HUGH   I could, but that would be unfriendly of me

WIFE   Unfriendly? I still don't understand

HUGH   It would be best to leave him alone and not tempt
him towards envy

WIFE   If you think so

HUGH   I know so

Spring will soon be here and then there will be
new flowers, fresh herbs and ripe cherries. I will
visit Little Hans then

*HANS is sitting in his house, wrapped in a quilt. He
is sleeping, but he mutters and sings and shivers. He
is dreaming of the spring and his garden. He is very
very cold. His silver buttons, pipe and chain are no
longer to be seen.*

GARETH   Plant the seeds
Pull up the weeds
Water the flowers
And prune the trees

He shivers and shivers.

And if I've nothing left to share
Will you be my friend?

LLINOS   Soon the winter passed, and the spring arrived.
Hans would get up early to plant his seeds and
look after his garden once again.

HUGH   Good morning Little Hans

HANS   Good morning Hugh

HUGH   And how have you been all winter?

HANS   It's very good of you to ask, very good indeed, but I'm afraid I had a very hard time of it, but now the spring has come and I am quite happy and all my flowers are doing well

HUGH   We often thought of you during the winter, Hans, and wondered how you were getting on

HANS   That was kind of you. I was afraid you had forgotten me

HUGH   Hans, I am surprised at you. A real friend never forgets. That is the most wonderful thing about friendship. How lovely your primroses are looking by the way

HANS   They certainly are very lovely this year, and I am fortunate to have so many of them

HUGH   You have indeed. So many

HANS   I am going to sell them in the market, and with the money I make I am going to buy back my wheelbarrow

HUGH   Buy back your wheelbarrow?

HANS   Yes

HUGH   You don't mean to say you have sold it? What a very silly thing to do

HANS   Well I had to

HUGH   Had to?

HANS   Yes. You see the winter was a very bad time for me and I had no money to buy bread

HUGH   So you sold your beautiful wheelbarrow?

HANS   Yes, I needed the money to buy food or I would have starved, so I sold my wheelbarrow, my silver buttons off my best coat, and my precious gold chain, but with the money I am going to make by selling my flowers I can buy them all back again

HUGH　Hans, dear Hans, my good friend Hans. I will give you my wheelbarrow. It is very old and needs repairing, the side is broken and the wheel needs mending, but in spite of all that, I will give it to you. I know it is very generous of me, but I think generosity is important in a friendship

HANS　Thank you so much my generous friend

HUGH　Besides, I have bought myself a new wheelbarrow

HANS　I can easily repair your old one. I have some wood in the house

HUGH　Some wood?

HANS　Yes

HUGH　Why, that is just what I want for the roof of my barn. There is a very large hole in it, and my corn would get wet if it rains. I need some wood to mend it

HANS　But

HUGH　No buts, dear Hans, it is only right that one good favour deserves another

HANS　But

HUGH　I am giving you my wheelbarrow, so you can give me the wood. Of course the wheelbarrow is worth far more than the wood, but our friendship is worth far more than the money

HANS　Of course

HUGH　Get me the wood at once, and I will start to work on my barn this very day

HANS Certainly

He gets the wood.

HUGH There's not much of it dear Hans

HANS It's all I have

HUGH I'm afraid that after I've mended my barn roof
there won't be any left for you to mend the
wheelbarrow

HANS Oh

HUGH But of course that is not my fault

HANS No

HUGH So as I am giving you my wheelbarrow I am sure
you would like to give me some primroses in
return

HANS But...

HUGH Here is the basket, mind you fill it quite full

HANS Quite full?

HUGH Well, really, as I have given you my wheelbarrow
I don't think that it is much to ask you for a few
flowers, do you?

HANS No

HUGH I should have thought friendship, true friendship
was quite free from selfishness of any kind

HANS My dear friend, my best friend, you are welcome
to all the flowers in my garden

HUGH Thank you so much

HANS I would much rather have your friendship than
my silver buttons, and gold chain anyday

HUGH How generous of you

HANS fills the basket with flowers.

HUGH   Goodbye Little Hans, my dear friend

HANS   Goodbye

The MILLER leaves.

HANS   Oh my. A new wheelbarrow

SONG OF THE GARDEN

HANS   Plant the seeds
Pull up the weeds
Water the flowers
And prune the trees

LLINOS   The next day the Miller's wife said to Hugh:

The MILLER enters carrying a large sack of flour.

WIFE   Where are you going, husband?

HUGH   I'm going to see my good friend Hans

WIFE   Are you taking the wheelbarrow?

HUGH   I can't take the wheelbarrow because I am taking
this heavy sack of flour

WIFE   You are so thoughtful, husband

HUGH leaves.

HANS   Friend friend will you be my friend?
On the hottest summer's day
Will you be my friend?
If I really need your help
Will you be my friend?
And if I've nothing left to share
Will you be my friend?

HUGH   Good morning dear friend Hans

HANS   Good morning Hugh on this fine day

HUGH   Are you busy?

HANS   Always busy dear friend

HUGH   Dear Little Hans, would you mind carrying this
        heavy sack of flour to the market for me?

HANS   Oh, I am so sorry, but I'm really very busy today.
        I have all my flowers to water and all my grass
        to mow

HUGH   Well, really, I think that considering that I am
        going to give you my wheelbarrow, it is rather
        unfriendly of you not to help me

HANS   Oh don't say that. I wouldn't be unfriendly for the
        whole world

HUGH   Well a true friend would help and take my flour to
        market for me

HANS   I am indeed a true friend, and I will stop what I
        am doing and take your flour to market

HUGH   Thank you dear Little Hans, you really do deserve
        my old wheelbarrow

        The MILLER exits.

HANS   Friend friend will you be my friend?
        Friend friend will you be my friend?
        Friend friend will you be my friend?

LLINOS So, Hans, being a true friend, stopped what he
        was doing and took the flour to market. As he
        walked along the long road, with his heavy load
        he dreamed about his new wheelbarrow. When
        he arrived home, tired and exhausted from the
        long journey he sat in his garden and watched
        the sun setting behind the hills

HANS   It really has been a hard day's work, but I am glad
        that I did not disappoint the Miller, for he is my
        best friend

SONG OF THE GARDEN

HANS   Plant the seeds
Pull up the weeds
Water the flowers
And trim the trees

And besides he is going to give me his
wheelbarrow. Tired now. Early night. Good
night birds. Good night garden

He sleeps.

LLINOS   The next day when the Miller arrived...

HUGH   Hans, Hans. Where are you little friend? Hans

HANS appears yawning and sleepy.

There you are. Upon my word you are very lazy.
Really, considering that I am going to give
you my wheelbarrow, I think you might work
harder. Laziness is wrong and I certainly don't
like any friends of mine to be lazy

HANS   But I worked so hard yesterday at the market that
I...

HUGH   I only say these things because you are my friend,
and friends must be honest with one another
and say exactly what they mean

HANS   Of course

HUGH   A true friend often has to say unpleasant things

HANS   I am sorry, but I was so tired that I thought that I
would lie in bed for a little time and listen to the
birds singing. I always work better after hearing
the birds sing

HUGH   Indeed. And do you have my money from the
flour?

HANS   Yes, indeed

HUGH   Now, I want you to come up to the Mill and mend
       my barn roof for me

HANS   Do you think it would be unfriendly of me if I said
       I was busy? Because I was at the market all day
       yesterday, I now have so much work to do in
       my garden

HUGH   Well really, I do not think it is much to ask of
       you, considering I am going to give you my
       wheelbarrow, but if you refuse I will have to do
       it myself

HANS   Oh, I will come and do it right away dear friend

LLINOS So Hans left his garden for another day and went
       up to the Mill to mend Hugh's roof. When he
       had finished it, which took all day, and was
       just about to go home to his garden, the Miller
       said...

HUGH   Have you mended the hole in the roof yet, Little
       Hans?

HANS   It is quite mended

HUGH   Ah, there is no work so delightful as the work that
       one does for others

HANS   You say such wonderful things, Hugh. I will never
       be able to have such great thought and ideas as
       you

HUGH   Perhaps one day, Little Hans, you will, but
       you must always practise thinking such great
       thoughts. Now you had better go home and rest,
       because tomorrow I want you to drive my sheep
       high up into the mountain

       He leaves.

HANS But my garden…

LLINOS So the next day Hans got up really early, said
goodbye to his garden and drove the Miller's
sheep high up into the mountains where the air
was clear and the grass was green and fresh.

HANS It is wonderful in the mountains, the air is so clear.
If Hugh had not asked me to drive his sheep, I
would have missed this glorious fresh clean air

LLINOS On his journey home, he thought of all the things
he was going to do in his garden the next day

SONG OF THE GARDEN

HANS I've got to
Plant the seeds
Pull up the weeds
Water the flowers
And prune the trees

LLINOS When he arrived home to his beautiful garden he
was so tired he fell asleep in the chair dreaming
about all the wonderful things he was going to
do next day in his garden

A storm starts to brew.

But a storm started to brew, and in the middle of
the night came a loud knock at the door
Knocking and knocking and knocking

HANS Who on earth can that be in the middle of such a
stormy night?

HUGH Hans! Hans!

HANS Hugh, whatever is wrong?

HUGH   Dear Little Hans, I am in great trouble. My wife
       has fallen off a ladder and hurt herself and I am
       going for the doctor

HANS   How can I help dear friend?

HUGH   The doctor lives so far away, would you go
       instead of me. As I am going to give you my
       wheelbarrow, I thought you would get the
       doctor for me

HANS   Certainly, I will go at once. It is so dark, will you
       lend me your lantern?

HUGH   I am very sorry Hans, it is my new lantern
       and it would be a great loss to me if anything
       happened to it

HANS   Never mind I will go without it

       The storm rages.

LLINOS It was a dreadful storm. The night was so dark that
       Little Hans could hardly see where he was going
       without a lantern to light his way. The wind was
       strong, the rain blew into his face and he could
       hardly stand. He was very brave and walked and
       walked until he arrived at the Doctor's house
       and knocked on the door

DOCTOR Who is there this time of night?

HANS   Little Hans, Doctor

DOCTOR What do you want Little Hans on such a stormy
       night?

HANS   The Miller's wife has fallen from a ladder and hurt
       herself, so the Miller needs you to come at once

DOCTOR Very well, I'll get my horse immediately

LLINOS   And off the doctor rode on her horse to rescue
          the Miller's wife. But the storm grew worse and
          worse. The rain was really heavy and Little
          Hans tried to find his way home but he could
          not see where he was going. It was so dark that
          he lost his way and wandered off the road onto
          the moors

HANS   Where am I? Where am I?

LLINOS   The wind blew in his face

HANS   I can't see where I am going. Help

LLINOS   The rain fell harder and harder

HANS   Help. Help

LLINOS   Little Hans tripped over a big rock and fell and
          fell and fell deep deep deep into the river.
          And drowned

          Pause.

          The next day, poor Little Hans' body was found
          floating in a great pool of water and was carried
          back to his cottage

HUGH   Poor Little Hans. I can't believe he is dead. He
          was such a devoted friend

LLINOS   He will certainly be a great loss to everybody. I
          will miss him

HUGH   A great loss to me at any rate. Why, I had as good
          as given him my wheelbarrow and now I don't
          really know what to do with it. It is very much in
          the way at home and it is in such bad repair that
          I could not get any money for it if I sold it. I will
          certainly take care not to give away anything
          again

LLINOS   Well really

HUGH   One certainly suffers from being generous

LLINOS   Nick

NICK   What?

LLINOS   That's it

NICK   That's what?

LLINOS   The end of my story

NICK   The end? But what am I going to do?

LLINOS   What?

NICK   Well, what am I going to do with my old wheelbarrow?

LLINOS   I don't believe you just said that. Have you learnt nothing from my story?

NICK   Yes, I have

LLINOS   What?

NICK   One certainly suffers from being generous

LLINOS   What do you mean?

NICK   Well, I promised Hans my wheelbarrow

LLINOS   Yes, but you never actually gave it to him

GARETH   Nick, you're not Hugh the Miller anymore, you're Nick

LLINOS   That's the end of my story

NICK   Oh! Great. Time for my story now

LLINOS   What did you think of the story?

NICK   Great. I loved being Hugh the Miller

GARETH   You were good

NICK   Yes, I thought so. He was such a good friend.

LLINOS   Do you really think so?

NICK   Oh yes, he was generous

LLINOS   Generous?

NICK   Absolutely. My story…

LLINOS   What did you think, Gareth?

GARETH   It was good

LLINOS   Did you enjoy being Hans

GARETH   Yes and no

LLINOS   Which bits did you enjoy?

GARETH   Working in the garden, growing the herbs and cherries. Oh, and listening to the birds

NICK   He was a wonderful gardener. Anyway, my story…

LLINOS   So which bits didn't you like?

NICK   Didn't like

GARETH   Oh lots

LLINOS   Tell me?

GARETH   Well
Being interrupted all the time

NICK   Are you saying I kept interrupting you?

GARETH   Well

LLINOS   Say it Gareth

GARETH   No, it doesn't matter

LLINOS   I think it does

GARETH   I'll just start clearing up all this mess

LLINOS   Gareth, say how you feel

GARETH   There's so much to do

LLINOS   Say it Gareth

NICK Leave him alone, Llinos, it was only a story

LLINOS Yes, but it had a point

NICK Why does everything have to have a point?

LLINOS You didn't get it did you, Nick?

NICK I did

LLINOS So, why did I tell the story then?

NICK To show how Hugh and Hans were such great friends

LLINOS Yes

NICK And to show how generous Hugh the Miller was

LLINOS Generous?

NICK Yes, generous, he was going to give Hans his wheelbarrow

GARETH And that's generous?

NICK Absolutely

LLINOS Generous?

NICK Oh, don't keep going on about it

GARETH Generous indeed. I'll tell you who was generous. I was

NICK How?

GARETH Little Hans gave you flowers. He gave you wood for the roof. He sold your flour in the market. He took your sheep up into the mountains. He went to fetch the doctor. And all because he was your friend and the promise of a wheelbarrow

NICK But he wanted to. That's how friendship works

GARETH I don't think so

NICK   Oh he did, but he also wanted to spend more time in his garden

GARETH   You see, Nick, you've turned into Hugh the Miller

NICK   What's wrong with that? He was a devoted friend to Hans

GARETH   Well, as a friend I think the Miller could have done a lot more

NICK   Like

GARETH   Like, like, like, not just taking the flowers

NICK   But Hans was happy to give them

LLINOS   Did you ever ask him?

GARETH   Did you ever say thank you for the wood? Did you ever offer to help him mend the roof? Did you say thank you for selling your flour? For taking your sheep up into the hills? For getting the doctor? No, they were all things you could have done yourself, or helped with, but you didn't

NICK   Did you ever say thank you for the wheelbarrow?

GARETH   I never got the wheelbarrow

NICK   That's not fair

GARETH   Fair!

LLINOS   It's hard you know, sometimes

GARETH   What is?

LLINOS   Being friends

NICK   You're absolutely right

LLINOS   I only told my story because you are my friend and friends must be honest with one another and say exactly what they mean

NICK   I said that in the story

LLINOS   I know and a true friend often has to say
                unpleasant things

NICK   I said that too

LLINOS   I know

NICK   But we are not in the story now

LLINOS   I know, but I'm still saying them as your friend.
                I'm being honest with you. Hugh the Miller was
                a bully

NICK   But

LLINOS   No buts about it

LLINOS   He was horrible to Hans

NICK   But he was his friend

LLINOS   Some friend

GARETH   Well, I don't want to be a friend like that. I want
                to be a proper friend. But I can't be a friend on
                my own

LLINOS   Well said Gareth

GARETH   Little Hans should have said that. He should have
                said no. He should have stood up for himself

NICK   But I'm your friend and friendship should be
                treasured.

LLINOS   It is the greatest thing in the world

GARETH   There is nothing greater. Friendship is about
                kindness

LLINOS   And caring

GARETH   And sharing

LLINOS   And trusting

GARETH   Being honest

LLINOS   Being loyal

NICK   And devoted to each other

LLINOS   On equal terms

GARETH   And if I were to play Hans again I would not let you get away with what you did Nick. I would say no

NICK   What do you mean?

GARETH   I would not let you bully me. I'd stand up for myself. I'd still be your friend, but I'd stand up for myself

NICK   But that wasn't me, Nick, that was Hugh the Miller saying that and sometimes, people don't know when they are being a bully

GARETH   So you agree then?

NICK   What?

GARETH   That Hugh was a bully?

NICK   Yes, I suppose so

GARETH   No suppose about it

NICK   If I were to play Hugh again, I would give you the lantern, so you would not get lost in the dark
But we're still friends aren't we?

GARETH   Of course

NICK   Great

LLINOS   Let's clear up all this stuff

NICK   Oh, I've got to go now

GARETH   Okay

LLINOS   Gareth

GARETH It's not okay is it?

NICK Look, I'll let you play my double bass if you clear
up my things for me

GARETH Like your 'wheelbarrow'

NICK What?

GARETH I'll give you my wheelbarrow if you mend my
roof

NICK Oh

GARETH You see, sometimes people don't know when they
are being a bully?

NICK I said that. Oh. I see

GARETH So

LLINOS So

GARETH So you can't go

NICK No

GARETH We have to all clear up the stuff

LLINOS Together

GARETH Because that's what friends do

NICK Look, let's not argue anymore

GARETH That's fine with me
I only say these things because you are my friend

LLINOS And friends must be honest with each other

NICK And say exactly what they mean

GARETH Exactly

LLINOS Exactly

NICK Exactly

LLINOS Nick?

NICK   Yes?

LLINOS   Tomorrow

NICK   Yes

LLINOS   Will you tell us one of your stories?

Pause.

NICK   Only if you'll help me

LLINOS /
GARETH   Great

LLINOS   Let's get going

GARETH   There's lots to do

NICK   We'll do it

ALL   Together

LLINOS   Because that's what good friends do

As they clear up the stage, they sing the final song of friendship.

Friend friend will you be my friend?
On the hottest summer's day
Will you be my friend?
If I really need your help
Will you be my friend?
And if I've nothing left to share
Will you be my friend?

Friend friend will you be my friend?
In the coldest winter
Will you be my friend?
Should I fall or lose my way
Will you be my friend?
And if I have no food that day
Will you be my friend?

Friend friend will you be my friend?
Friend friend will you be my friend?
Friend friend will you be my friend?

END

THE HAPPY PRINCE

Characters

Actor 1   JAN, a young child who lives in the south of the town
          and has a bad cough
          MAYOR
          MIKA'S FATHER

Actor 2   JO, a young child who lives in the east of the town and
          is very unhappy
          COUNCILLOR 1
          JAN'S MOTHER

Actor 3   MIKA, a young child who lives in the west of the town
          and sells matches
          COUNCILLOR 2
          JO'S MOTHER

All play   THE HAPPY PRINCE, represented by a human-size
          puppet

          THE SWALLOW, represented by a rod puppet

The Happy Prince was first performed by The Sherman Theatre Company on 27 October 2006 with the following company:

ACTOR 1, Mark Carlisle
ACTOR 2, Nia Lynn
ACTOR 3, Llinos Mai

Director Phil Clark
Designer Tina Reeves
Lighting Designer Ceri James
Composer / Musical Director Lucy Rivers
Stage Managers Brenda Knight & Kate Borde

A square performance area represents the Town Square in the north of the town. It is decorated for the joyous occasion of the unveiling of the statue of the Happy Prince.

In Corner 1 stands the statue of the Happy Prince, covered with a cloth.

In Corner 2 is the home of Jan.

In Corner 3 is the home of Jo.

In Corner 4 is the home of Mika.

The audience are welcomed to the performance space by the actors.

MIKA, a little match seller, sells matches and sings a song.

SONG OF THE LITTLE MATCH SELLER

MIKA Matches
Matches
Please buy my matches

Matches for your candles
In the dark to give you light
Matches for your lanterns
To guide you through the night

Matches
Matches
Please buy my matches

Matches to light your fires
To keep you safe and warm
Matches for your lamplight
And shelter from the storm

Matches
Matches
Please buy my matches

A fanfare sounds. Enter the COUNCILLORS and the LORD MAYOR.

COUNCILLOR 1 Good citizens all,
Welcome to this important occasion.
The official unveiling…

LORD MAYOR by the Lord Mayor…

COUNCILLOR 2 …by his Lordship The Lord Mayor…

COUNCILLOR 1 …of the Statue of

BOTH The Happy Prince.

COUNCILLOR 1 Please welcome His Lordship

COUNCILLOR 2 His magnificent Lordship.

BOTH Our Lord Mayor.

MAYOR Good citizens all.

COUNCILLOR 1 That's what I said

MAYOR Thank you, Councillor.
Good Citizens All. Welcome to this important
occasion. This is an important and magnificent
day for us all, and before I unveil the beautiful
new golden statue, I'd like to recite this poem
that I've written for this important occasion.

COUNCILLOR 1 Quiet please

COUNCILLOR 2 Pray silence for his worship the Lord Mayor's
Poem.

COUNCILLOR 1 The Lord Mayor's Poem.

MAYOR Silence please.

THE LORD MAYOR'S POEM

Oh yea
Oh yea
Oh yea
This is a very important day.

We'll show the statue
We hope you'll say thank you,
Oh yea
Oh yea
Oh yea.

In life our Prince was so happy
A very important chappie
He sang like a bird
You heard every word
There's no doubting he was joyously happy

Oh yea
Oh yea
Oh yea
This is a very important day.

Now that our Prince is dead
We've a statue of him instead
It stands there so bold
All covered in gold
But inside he's all made of lead.

He may not be all he appears
But he's covered in gold my dears
We've made him look grand
The best in the land
So come on give him three cheers.

The statue is unveiled.

MAYOR   Hip pip

COUNCILLORS   Horah

MAYOR   Hip pip

COUNCILLORS   Horah

MAYOR   Hip pip

COUNCILLORS   Horah

Applause.

MAYOR   Isn't he fine.

COUNCILLOR 1   Isn't he grand.

COUNCILLOR 2   Isn't he magnificent.

MAYOR   So golden.

COUNCILLOR 1   So regal.

COUNCILLOR 2   So royal.

COUNCILLOR 2   This is a happy occasion.

MAYOR   Our golden Happy Prince never cried for anything.

COUNCILLORS   Never.

COUNCILLOR 1   He is beautiful.

COUNCILLOR 2   Gloriously beautiful.

COUNCILLOR 1   With sapphires for eyes.

COUNCILLOR 2   Sparkling sapphires.

MAYOR   All the way from India. He is magnificent.

COUNCILLOR 1   Covered in gold.

COUNCILLOR 2   All over.

COUNCILLOR 1   A red ruby in his sword.

COUNCILLOR 2   Expensive.

MAYOR   No expense spared.

COUNCILLOR 1   A truly magnificent statue.

MAYOR   We will remember our Prince always.

COUNCILLORS   Always.

COUNCILLOR 1   He is as beautiful as a weather cock.

COUNCILLOR 2   Only not quite as useful.
I think he's more like an angel.

COUNCILLOR 1 Have you ever seen an angel?

COUNCILLOR 2 Yes. In my dreams.

MAYOR I'm glad there is someone in the world who is happy.

COUNCILLORS Here, here.

MAYOR And now we must sing our Anthem.

COUNCILLOR 1 In praise of the Prince.

COUNCILLOR 2 Of the Happy Prince.

MAYOR Are we all ready?

ANTHEM TO THE HAPPY PRINCE

This is an action song. The company sing the song, and then teach it to the audience with the actions.

Our Prince
Our Happy Prince
Standing high above

Our Prince
Our Happy Prince
Your heart so full of love

Our Prince
Our Happy Prince
Why did you so depart?

Our Prince
Our Happy Prince
Stay for ever in our hearts

Applause.

MAYOR A very enjoyable ceremony.

COUNCILLOR 1 An excellent speech Lord Mayor.

MAYOR Why was that child crying?

COUNCILLOR 1 And another coughing?

MAYOR Children? Coughing! Crying! Why do they have
to ruin everything?

*The LORD MAYOR bumps into MIKA the little match
seller, and pushes her matches all over the floor.*

Stupid child. Get out of my way.
Don't you know who I am?

COUNCILLOR 1 Don't you know who he is?

*The MAYOR and COUNCILLORS leave. MIKA is
picking up the matches. She is alone in the square.
She stares at the statue. She approaches the statue. It
is now dusk.*

SONG OF THE LITTLE MATCH SELLER

MIKA Matches
Matches
Who will buy my matches

Matches for your candles
In the dark to give you light
Matches for your lanterns
To guide you through the night

Matches
Matches
Who will buy my matches

End of song.

Hello Happy Prince.
What's it like to be happy all the time?
Tell me? Please!
Can I be happy all the time? My name is Mika
and I was selling matches, here in the square.
Can you see me? Could you, with your beautiful
sparkling eyes?

But the mayor pushed me and I dropped the
  matches.
Did you see?
They fell into a puddle of water. They are ruined
  and no one will want to buy them.
Can you see me?
My father will punish me for being so clumsy.
I'm frightened to go home.
Oh Happy Prince, I wish you could help me.
I wish.
I wish.

There is a noise. A cough.

What's that? Maybe it's my father.
I'll hide.

She hides.
JAN walks into the square and stares at the statue.
He coughs.

JAN You are beautiful.
  Very beautiful.
  (*Coughs.*)
  You are happy.
  Very happy.
  (*Coughs.*)
  I wish I could be happy
  As happy as you.
  Happy all the time.
  My name is Jan,
  But I'm not well, and we can't afford the medicine
    to make me better.
  If only I had enough money to buy the medicine,
    perhaps then I would be happy,
  Like you.
  (*Coughs.*)

If only.

If only.

There is a noise. JAN hides.

JO walks into the square and stares at the statue with wonder. She cries and sings. JO gets closer. She extends her hand towards the PRINCE.

JO   It's like the moon.

If only I could touch the moon.

Oh Happy Prince,

I want to be happy like you. My name is Jo

But it is so cold in our house

It just makes me miserable.

(*Cries.*)

If we had enough money to buy more wood for
    the fire we would be warm and not miserable all
    the time.

(*Cries.*)

If we were warm my mother could write her
    stories and we could sell them.

She will, one day. It's my dream.

In my dream we are warm and cosy and happy,
    just like you.

What do you think Happy Prince?

Your eyes are like the moon

Full of light and strength.

I want the moon.

I want the moon.

I dream.

I dream.

(*Cries.*)

JAN enters the square.

JAN   Why are you crying?

JO   For the moon.

MIKA enters the square.

MIKA You can't cry for the moon.

JO I can.

JAN But why are you crying for the moon?

JO I want the moon.

MIKA But you can't have the moon.

JO Why not?

JAN It belongs to all of us.

MIKA Like the sun.

JAN And the stars.

MIKA And the night.

JAN And the day.

JO But we are so poor. I just want the moon.

MIKA Well you can't have it.

JO cries.

JAN Because it's mine.

MIKA And mine.

JO MINE.

JAN Yes, yours.

ALL Ours.

The SWALLOW flies over. They look up.

MIKA Were you invited to the ceremony?

JO No. Were you?

MIKA No.

JAN Nor me, but I watched it from afar.

JO I saw you talking to the statue.

JAN So?

MIKA   I saw you talking to the statue.

JO   Isn't he beautiful?

JAN   Isn't he happy?

MIKA   Yes.

JO   He looks like he's got the moon.

ALL   For ever.

JAN   And anyway, what's wrong with talking to the statue?

JO   Nothing.

JAN   Well.

JO   I never said there was anything wrong with it.

JAN   You did it.

JO   Yes.

MIKA   And you did it.

JAN   Yes.

MIKA   And I did it.

JAN   We all did it.

JO   We all talked to the Happy Prince.

The SWALLOW flies over. They look up.

MIKA   The birds are flying to the warm lands.

JAN   They must.

JO   Or they will die from the cold here in winter.

Beat.

MIKA   Who are you?

JAN   My name is Jan and I live on the south side.

MIKA   Who are you?

JO   My name is Jo and I live in the east.

JO / JAN Who are you?

MIKA My name is Mika and I live in the west.

ALL North.

JAN South.

JO East.

MIKA West.

JAN No wonder we've never met before.

They laugh.

JO I want to be like the Happy Prince.

MIKA And me.

JAN And me.

JO I want to be happy.

JAN / MIKA All the time.

ALL For ever.

JO I wonder what it's like to be happy all the time?

MIKA I wonder what it's like to be happy for ever?

JAN If I could make you happy I would.

JO If I could make you happy I would.

MIKA If I could make you happy I would.

JAN I'd make you happy all the time.

JO For ever.

MIKA Every day the sun would shine.

JAN And every night the moon would rise.

JO I wouldn't feel cold.

MIKA I wouldn't be frightened.

JAN I wouldn't be ill.

JO Because every day the sun would shine.

JAN   And every night the moon would rise.

MIKA   And we would all be happy.

JAN   Happy in our hearts.

ALL   All of the time.

MIKA   I wish.

JAN   If only.

JO   I dream.

The SWALLOW flies over. They look up.

ALL   Goodbye Swallows

JO   I didn't feel cold.

MIKA   I didn't feel frightened.

JAN   I didn't feel ill.

JO   Cos I'd make you happy.

MIKA   Happy in your heart.

JO   All of the time.
And every night the moon would rise.

JAN   And every day the sun would shine.

JO   I didn't feel cold

JAN   Or ill

MIKA   Or frightened

ALL   Happy in our hearts, all the time.

CHILD'S THEME SONG

ALL   And every night the moon would rise.
And every day the sun would shine
I wouldn't feel cold
Or ill
Or frightened

Happy in our hearts
All the time.

And every night the moon would rise.
And every day the sun would shine
I wouldn't feel cold
Or ill
Or frightened
Happy in our hearts
All the time.

Song ends.

MIKA I wish.

JAN If only.

JO I dream.

JAN It's getting dark.

MIKA I have to go.

JO Me too.

JAN To the south.

JO To the east.

MIKA To the west.

JAN Remember.

MIKA I wish.

JAN If only.

JO I dream. Goodbye Jan.

MIKA Goodbye Jo.

JAN Goodbye Mika.

ALL Remember me.

MIKA I wish.

JAN If only.

JO I dream.

The three children leave.

It is now night-time.
A FLOCK OF SWALLOWS flies into the square.
They are on their way to the warm lands, emigrating.

FLOCK Warm lands
Oh the warm lands
Where the tall birds stand
On the banks of the river
Catching fish
Catching fish

Ah the warm lands
Now we must fly
Over the seas
And far away

SWALLOW It's a long flight south

A SWALLOW But it will be beautifully warm

SWALLOW A holiday in the sun

BOTH Wohoo

A SWALLOW I can't wait to get there

SWALLOW There'll be camels

A SWALLOW And snakes

SWALLOW And butterflies

A SWALLOW And honey cakes

BOTH Over the seas and far away

SONG OF THE SWALLOW'S FLIGHT

FLOCK North, south, east, west
Over the town I fly

North, south, east, west
High up in the sky

North, south, east, west
Over the town I fly
North, south, east, west
Flying so high

SWALLOW   I'm a bit tired

FLOCK   Come on

SWALLOW   I need a rest

FLOCK   Keep flying

SWALLOW   I'll catch you up

A SWALLOW   We'll be waiting

SWALLOW   I shall put up, here

FLOCK   See you in the warm lands

SWALLOW   This is a fine position with plenty of fresh air
I have a golden bedroom

*The SWALLOW settles at the foot of the HAPPY
PRINCE.*
It makes itself comfortable. It sleeps.
The statue moves.

Jan's house in the south of the town:

JAN   Mother I'm home (*Coughs.*)

MOTHER   You're coughing really badly.

JAN   I saw the Happy Prince. He was tall and golden
and happy. (*Coughs.*)

MOTHER   You must rest.

JAN   He was wonderful.

MOTHER   Like you.

JAN   What do you mean?

MOTHER   You are my happy prince. If only I had enough money, I would buy you more medicine.

JAN   If only. Am I really?

MOTHER   Really what?

JAN   Your happy prince.

MOTHER   Yes, and you always will be.

JAN   For ever.

MOTHER   And ever. If only.

They hug – JAN coughs.

Now bed.

Jo's house in the east of the town.

JO   Mother I'm home.

MOTHER   It's so cold.

JO   I saw the Happy Prince. He was tall and golden and happy.

MOTHER   Have you been crying?

JO   He was beautiful.

MOTHER   And warm in his coat of gold.

JO   Oh mother, let me hug you warm.

MOTHER   It's so cold, I can't write anymore.

JO   I dream that we will one day be so warm and you will be able to write your stories again.

MOTHER   And I would write you a story that would make you smile and make you feel warm and golden.

JO   One day.

MOTHER Yes one day, and we will be over the moon. Now
        bed.

Mika's house in the west of the town.

MIKA Father I'm home.

FATHER How much money did you make?

MIKA I saw the Happy Prince, he was tall and golden
      and happy.

FATHER I said how much money did you make?

MIKA I wish I could be tall and golden and…

FATHER How much?

MIKA None.

FATHER None.

MIKA I dropped the matches. Well, the Lord Mayor
      pushed…

FATHER What?

MIKA They are ruined, but I saw the Prince.

FATHER How are we going to live with no money?

MIKA I'm sorry.

FATHER Sorry!
        Go to bed.

MIKA But…

FATHER No buts, get to bed now.

        *JAN, JO and MIKA all open their bedroom windows
        at the same time.*

MIKA I wish.

JAN If only.

JO I dream.

THE WARM LANDS

ALL   In the warm lands
Where the tall birds stand
On the banks of the river
Catching fish

In the warm lands
Where I must fly
Over the seas
and far away

In the warm lands
Where the camels walk
Side by side through the desert
Bearing gifts to the king of the moon

In the warm lands
Where I belong

SWALLOW   I have a Golden Bedroom

The Town Square:
It is early morning. The SWALLOW is asleep at the
feet of the HAPPY PRINCE.
The PRINCE starts to cry. Tears drop onto the sleeping
SWALLOW. The SWALLOW wakes.

Oh no.
Rain.
I'm going to get soaked. That's strange. It's only
    raining here, where I am.
Everywhere else is dry.

PRINCE   It's not rain.

SWALLOW   Who was that?

PRINCE   Me.

SWALLOW   Who's me, there's only me here.

PRINCE   The statue.

SWALLOW   The statue.

PRINCE   Yes, the Happy Prince, and they are my sad tears.

SWALLOW   Statues can't cry.

PRINCE   I can.

SWALLOW   But you're supposed to be a Happy Prince. You've quite drenched me, I'm soaked.

PRINCE   Sorry.

SWALLOW   Why are you crying?

PRINCE   Because the children are so unhappy.

SWALLOW   What children?

PRINCE   The children in the town.

SWALLOW   Sorry Prince, I have to go.

PRINCE   No. Don't go. Please little swallow.

SWALLOW   I must go. Winter is coming and I must fly over the seas and far away to the warm lands, where the sun is shining. Where the tall birds stand in long rows on the banks of the warm river and catch golden fish in their beaks. Where the camels walk slowly side by side through the deserts carrying beautiful gifts to the King of the Mountains of the moon. Over the seas and far away in the warm lands I must go. I must keep warm or I will die.

PRINCE   Of course little swallow, but will you help me before you fly away?

SWALLOW   How can I help you?

PRINCE   In the south side of the town lives the little boy Jan.

He has a terrible cough, but his mother can't
    afford to buy him medicine because they are so
    poor.
Swallow, swallow, little swallow. Take the red ruby
    out of my sword. My feet are fastened to the
    pedestal and I cannot move. Take the ruby to
    Jan.

SWALLOW   But my friends and family are waiting for me in
    the warm lands.

PRINCE   Swallow, swallow, little swallow, will you not stay
    with me one night and be my messenger? Jan is
    so ill and his mother so sad.
This ruby is worth nothing to me up here, but
    with the ruby Jan and his mother can buy new
    medicine and he will be well again.

SWALLOW   It is very cold here (and wet) but I will stay with
    you one night only and be your messenger.

PRINCE   Thank you, thank you little swallow, now take the
    ruby –

The SWALLOW takes the ruby.

– and in the dead of night fly to little Jan's house
    in the south of the town. But, whatever happens,
    don't be seen.
Now fly, fly, fly.

SONG OF THE SWALLOW'S FLIGHT

SWALLOW   North, south, east, west
    Over the town I fly
    North, south, east, west
    High up in the sky

    North, south, east, west
    Over the town I fly

North, south, east, west
Flying so high

The SWALLOW arrives at JAN's house. He is asleep. He is restless and coughing. The SWALLOW flies in and places the ruby on his bed. The SWALLOW fans JAN's face with its wings. The SWALLOW retreats. JAN stirs.

JAN How cool I feel. I must be getting better.

JAN sees the ruby.

Wow!
Mother, mother!

The SWALLOW flies off.

SONG OF THE SWALLOW'S FLIGHT

SWALLOW North, south, east, west
Over the town I fly.
North, south, east, west
High up in the sky

North, south, east, west
Over the town I fly
North, south, east, west
Flying so high.

*The Town Square. Daytime.
The SWALLOW arrives.*

PRINCE Welcome, welcome little swallow. Was your mission successful?

SWALLOW It was, and it's quite curious.

PRINCE What do you mean?

SWALLOW But I feel quite warm now, although it is still cold.

PRINCE   That is because you have done a good thing and
           your heart is full.

SWALLOW   Of what?

PRINCE   Of love, and happiness. Thank you.

SWALLOW   I am tired, but tonight I must fly over the seas and
           far away to the warm lands. The winter here is
           getting colder and I could die from the cold.

PRINCE   Swallow, swallow, little swallow, will you not stay
           with me one more night?

SWALLOW   But I am waited for by my friends and family in
           the warm lands.

PRINCE   Swallow, swallow, little swallow. In the east of the
           town I see a small child, Jo, and she is crying for
           the moon. She is so cold she cannot afford wood
           for the fire. She and her mother are so cold and
           really hungry.

SWALLOW   I will wait with you one night longer.

PRINCE   You have a beautiful heart.

SWALLOW   Shall I take her another ruby?

PRINCE   Alas! I have no ruby now. My eyes are all that I
           have left. They are made of rare sapphires which
           were brought from India a thousand years ago.

SWALLOW   Wow.

PRINCE   Pluck out one of my sapphires and take it to little
           Jo.

SWALLOW   Dear Prince, I cannot do that.

PRINCE   Yes, you must. Then Jo won't need to cry for the
           moon anymore.

SWALLOW   But Prince –

PRINCE Swallow, swallow, little swallow, do as I command
you.

The SWALLOW takes the sapphire.

Take this sapphire and in the dead of night fly to
Jo's house in the east of the town. But, whatever
happens, don't be seen.
Now fly, fly, fly.

SONG OF THE SWALLOW'S FLIGHT

SWALLOW North, south, east, west
Over the town I fly.
North, south, east, west
High up in the sky

North, south, east, west
Flying up on high
North, south, east, west
Flying so high.

Jo's house in the east of the town:
JO is crying in her sleep.
The SWALLOW flies in and leaves the sapphire on the
foot of the bed. The SWALLOW brushes JO's face with
its wings. JO stops crying. The SWALLOW retreats.

JO What was that?

She sees the sapphire.

The moon, I've got the moon. Mother, mother,
It's the moon. A beautiful sapphire.
Yes, just like the moon. We can buy firewood, and
food, and you can finish writing your story. And
we can sell your story. We'll be over the moon.
Mother, mother.

She exits.

SONG OF THE SWALLOW'S FLIGHT

SWALLOW North, south, east, west
Over the town I fly.
North, south, east, west
High up in the sky

North, south, east, west
Over the town I fly
North, south, east, west
Flying so high.

The Town Square
The SWALLOW arrives.

PRINCE Swallow, swallow, little swallow. Was your mission
successful?

SWALLOW Yes Happy Prince. And now I must bid you
farewell.

PRINCE Swallow, swallow, little swallow. Will you not stay
with me one night longer?

SWALLOW It is winter and the cold snows will soon be here.
Dear Prince, I must leave you for the warm lands
over the seas and far away. I will never forget
you.
Next spring, when I return, I will bring you back
two beautiful jewels from the warm lands to
replace those you have given away.

PRINCE You are so kind. You have a kind heart.

SWALLOW The ruby shall be redder than a red rose and the
sapphire as beautiful as the moon.

PRINCE But swallow, swallow, little swallow, in the west of
the town there is a little match girl called Mika.
She has dropped her matches in the wet gutter
and they are all ruined. Her father is very angry,

and if Mika doesn't sell her matches, her father
will beat her.

SWALLOW   What can I do to stop such cruelty?

PRINCE   Pluck out my other eye and take it to Mika. Then
her father will not beat her.

SWALLOW   I will stay with you one night longer. But I cannot
pluck out your eye, you will be quite blind.

PRINCE   Swallow, swallow, little swallow, do as I
command.

The SWALLOW plucks out the sapphire.

And in the dead of night fly to Mika the little
match girl's house in the west of the town.
But, whatever happens, don't be seen.
Now fly, fly, fly.

SONG OF THE SWALLOW'S FLIGHT

SWALLOW   North, south, east, west
Over the town I fly.
North, south, east, west
High up in the sky

North, south, east, west
Over the town I fly
North, south, east, west
Flying so high.

Mika's house in the west of the town:
MIKA is blowing on the matches to dry them.

MIKA   My matches are so damp and wet, no one will
ever buy them. My father will beat me if I don't
sell my matches and make him some money.

The SWALLOW flies in – unseen – and drops the
sapphire.

What was that?

MIKA investigates. As she does the SWALLOW flaps its wings over the matches. MIKA finds the sapphire.

It's a beautiful jewel. A sapphire, I think. Just like…
Father, father.

FATHER Are those matches dry?

MIKA (*She looks with amazement.*) Yes, completely dry.

FATHER So get them sold.

MIKA But father, look.

FATHER (*Off.*) No buts. Get to the town square and sell those matches – or there will be no tea.

MIKA But the sapphire… I must tell Jo and Jan. Jo… Jan…

She puts it in her pocket and leaves.

SONG OF THE SWALLOW'S FLIGHT

SWALLOW North, south, east, west
Over the town I fly.
North, south, east, west
High up in the sky

North, south, east, west
Over the town I fly.
North, south, east, west
Flying so high.

The Town Square.
The SWALLOW arrives.

PRINCE Was your mission successful?

SWALLOW Yes.

PRINCE   Were you seen?

SWALLOW   No.

PRINCE   Well done.

SWALLOW   You are blind Happy Prince, so I will stay with
you always.

PRINCE   No, little swallow, you must fly over the seas and
far away to the warm lands.

SWALLOW   I will stay with you always.

PRINCE   But what about the warm lands?

SWALLOW   Ah, the warm lands,
Over the seas and far away
In the warm lands.

PRINCE   Dear swallow,
You are indeed a great true friend.

SWALLOW   And I will stay with you always.

PRINCE   How great is the power of true love.
Swallow, swallow, little swallow, now I am blind,
fly over our great town and tell me what you see
with your eyes. Fly high. Fly strong.

The SWALLOW flies high into the sky.

SWALLOW   I see the rich people making merry in their
beautiful houses. I see the poor people hungry
and starving. I see the faces of the starving
children, crying. I see two little children, under
the river bridge, so hungry and cold they are
hugging each other to keep warm. I see...

PRINCE   Enough, enough, little swallow. Such pictures
make my heart ache and surely it will break with
such poverty. And I am covered in rich gold.

Swallow, swallow, little swallow, you must take off all my gold, leaf by leaf, and give it to my poor people. It is nearly deep winter and the snows are coming. Do it now little swallow. Do it now.

The SWALLOW starts to lift off all the gold from the PRINCE and distribute it throughout the town.

The statue of the HAPPY PRINCE is stripped of all his gold. The SWALLOW returns.

PRINCE   Thank you little swallow, you have a beautiful heart that is full of love.

SWALLOW   I am cold, so, so cold, and I haven't the strength to fly to the warm lands, so I will stay with you for ever. Happy Prince, will you let me kiss your hand?
(*He does so.*)
Goodbye dear Prince. Goodbye.

PRINCE   I am glad that you are going to the warm land over the seas and far away.

SWALLOW   I am not going to the warm lands. I am going for ever to the house of the long sleep.
(*He kisses the PRINCE.*)
Goodbye dear Prince.
Goodbye.
For ever.

The SWALLOW dies at the foot of the PRINCE and a loud crack is heard as the PRINCE cries out.

PRINCE   For ever.

The Town Square. The next morning.
The MAYOR and two COUNCILLORS enter.

MAYOR   Dear me. How shabby and ugly the Prince looks.

COUNCILLOR 1 How shabby indeed.

COUNCILLOR 2 Extremely ugly.

COUNCILLOR 1 Little better than a beggar.

MAYOR And there is a dead bird at its feet.

COUNCILLOR 1 How disgusting.

COUNCILLOR 2 Extremely disgusting.

MAYOR We really must make a law that birds are not allowed to die in the town square.

COUNCILLOR 1 It will be done immediately.

COUNCILLOR 2 Immediately.

MAYOR And as the statue of the Happy Prince is no longer beautiful he is no longer useful.

COUNCILLOR 1 No longer beautiful.

COUNCILLOR 2 No longer useful.

MAYOR Pull it down. Pull it down.

COUNCILLOR 1 Pull it down.

COUNCILLOR 2 Pull it down.

They start pulling down the statue.

MAYOR Take it to the furnace and melt it down.

COUNCILLOR 1 To the furnace.

COUNCILLOR 2 Melt it down.

MAYOR And burn that dead bird.

COUNCILLOR 2 Burn it.

COUNCILLOR 1 Burn it.

MAYOR We must have another statue of course.

COUNCILLOR 1 Of course.

COUNCILLOR 2 Of course.

MAYOR   And it shall be a statue of…

COUNCILLOR 1   Me, your worship?

COUNCILLOR 2   Me, your worship?

MAYOR   Of myself of course.

COUNCILLOR 1   Of course.

COUNCILLOR 2   Of course.

The MAYOR and COUNCILLORS leave.
JAN, JO and MIKA enter the square.

JO   Jan.

MIKA   Jo.

JAN   Mika.

JO   Have you heard?

MIKA   Yes.

JAN   It can't be true.

MIKA   It is.

ALL   Look.

They sing:

ANTHEM TO THE HAPPY PRINCE

ALL   Our Prince
Our Happy Prince
Standing high above

Our Prince
Our Happy Prince
Your heart so full of love

Our Prince
Our Happy Prince
Why did you so depart?

End of song.

JO The Happy Prince has gone.

MIKA Destroyed.

JAN For ever.

JO Because they thought he was no longer beautiful.

MIKA But he will always be beautiful to me.

JAN And me.

JO He will be beautiful in my heart.

MIKA Yes, in my heart I will always love him.

JAN He may be gone.

JO But he will never be forgotten.

Beat.

JAN You're not crying.

JO No.

MIKA And you're not coughing.

JAN No.

JO And you're not frightened any more.

MIKA No.

JO I've got the moon.

JAN And I've got the moon.

MIKA And I've got the moon.

They open the palms of their hands and there are the ruby and sapphires.

It's for you.

JO It's for you.

JAN It's for you.

They give each other their jewels.

ALL It's for your happiness.

*All three look to where the HAPPY PRINCE was,
knowingly. They make bird wings with their hands
and their birds fly away.*

For ever.

They sing:

DON'T CRY FOR THE MOON

Don't cry for the moon
Look deep inside your heart
Don't cry for the moon
True love will never part

Follow your dreams
To the north, south, east and west
Imagine keep on dreaming
It's a long and happy quest

Don't cry for the moon
Look deep inside your heart
Don't cry for the moon
True love will never part

Follow your dreams
To the North, South, East and West
Imagine keep on dreaming
It's a long and happy quest

So don't cry for the moon
Look deep inside your heart
Never cry for the moon
True love will never part

MIKA I wish.

JAN If only.

JO I dream.

END

THE SELFISH GIANT

Characters

Actor 1 GERAINT
         GIANT
         JULIA'S MUM
         THE NORTH WIND

Actor 2 JULIA
         KEITH'S GRANDAD
         THE BOY
         FROST

Actor 3 KEITH
         GERAINT'S DAD
         SNOW

The story is set in a large garden. Throughout the play, the narration can be spoken by all three actors chorally or individually.

The Selfish Giant was first performed by The Sherman Theatre Company on 13 October 2005 with the following company:

ACTOR 1, Nick Wayland Evans
ACTOR 2, Rhiannon Meades
ACTOR 3, Ben Harrison

Director Phil Clark
Designer Tina Reeves
Lighting Designer Ceri James
Composer / Musical Director Lucy Rivers
Stage Managers Sasha Dobbs & Sharlene Harvard Young

GERAINT, JULIA and KEITH welcome the audience into the garden. They seem at home in the garden. It's where they want to be. They care for the garden and all that is in it.

GERAINT Right! I'll begin.

JULIA Oh! I thought I'd begin.

KEITH I wanted to begin.

GERAINT (*Beginning.*) Hallo.

JULIA I said I'd begin (*Beginning.*) Hallo.

KEITH I wanted to begin (*Beginning.*) Hallo.

ALL Hallo.

GERAINT Welcome.

JULIA Welcome.

KEITH Welcome.

GERAINT Welcome

JULIA to our

KEITH true

ALL story.

GERAINT It happened when we were young.

JULIA Very young.

KEITH Very, very, very young.

GERAINT It happened here in this garden.

JULIA A long time ago.

KEITH When we made a promise.

GERAINT For ever.

JULIA And for ever.

KEITH And for ever.

At this point GERAINT, JULIA and KEITH make a physical pact, a promise, a bond with their hands.

SONG

(*Chorus.*) Welcome welcome welcome
Our story we will tell
Welcome welcome welcome
We hope you're good and well.

Our story really happened
A long long time ago
It's important that we tell it
Get comfy, cos here we go.

Sometimes our story's happy
Sometimes our story's sad.
Sometimes it's quite funny
And sometimes very bad.

Welcome welcome welcome
Our story we will tell
Welcome welcome welcome
We hope you're good and well.

Our story's not made up
Our story it is true
And the most important thing of all
Is to tell it just for you.

So
Welcome welcome welcome
Our story we will tell
Welcome welcome welcome
We hope you're good and well.

GERAINT   (*Remembering.*) Our story today is about
                a Giant.

JULIA   (*Remembering.*) A Selfish Giant.

KEITH   (*Remembering.*) A very Selfish Giant

GERAINT   who once owned this big, beautiful garden.

JULIA and all fruit trees

KEITH and all flowers

GERAINT and all the...

JULIA But our story really begins

KEITH With us.

GERAINT Geraint.

JULIA Julia.

KEITH Keith.

GERAINT When we were young.

JULIA Very young.

KEITH Very, very, very young.

SONG

Welcome welcome welcome
Our story we will tell
Welcome welcome welcome
We hope you're good and well.

GERAINT I'm Geraint.

JULIA I'm Julia.

GERAINT /
JULIA and...

KEITH I'm Keith.

GERAINT Hi.

JULIA Hi.

KEITH Hi.

JULIA Coming out to play?

KEITH Yeah.

GERAINT And me.

DAD (*Shouts.*) Geraint!

GERAINT Yes, Dad?

DAD Can you come and help me please?

GERAINT I can't.

DAD Why not?

GERAINT I'm busy.

DAD Busy?

GERAINT Yes, busy. I'm making something.

DAD Making what?

GERAINT Something.

MUM (*Shouts.*) Julia!

JULIA Yes, Mum.

MUM Have you tidied your room?

JULIA Not yet.

MUM Why not?

JULIA I'm busy.

MUM Busy?

JULIA Yes, busy. I'm writing something.

MUM Writing what?

JULIA Something.

GRANDAD (*Shouts.*) Keith!

KEITH Yes, Grandad.

GRANDAD Can you run to the shop for me?

KEITH Not now, Grandad.

GRANDAD Why not?

KEITH I'm busy.

GRANDAD Busy?

KEITH Yes, busy. I'm practising.

GRANDAD Practising what?

KEITH My music.

GRANDAD I can't hear anything.

MUM (*Shouts.*) Julia!

DAD (*Shouts.*) Geraint!

MUM Have you seen Julia?

GRANDAD No. Keith?

DAD No. Geraint?

MUM Where have these children gone?

DAD I wish I knew.

GRANDAD Never here when you want them.

GRANDAD /
MUM / DAD Kids, eh!

GRANDAD (*Shouts.*) Keith! (*Exits.*)

MUM (*Shouts.*) Julia! (*Exits.*)

DAD (*Shouts.*) Geraint! (*Exits.*)

KEITH (*Whispering.*) Hi Julia.

JULIA (*Whispering.*) Hi Keith.

JULIA / KEITH (*Whispering*) Hi Geraint.

GERAINT Hi. That was close.

GERAINT /
JULIA / KEITH Parents, eh!

JULIA Where shall we play?

KEITH Not in the street. It's dangerous.

JULIA What are you making?

GERAINT Something.

KEITH Let's see then.

GERAINT What are you writing?

JULIA A poem.

KEITH Where?

JULIA In my head.

GERAINT Prove it.

JULIA You said you were practising your music.

KEITH I was.

GERAINT Didn't hear you.

DAD (*Off.*) Geraint!

MUM (*Off.*) Julia!

GRANDAD (*Off.*) Keith!

GERAINT
JULIA / KEITH Parents!

JULIA Quick, run for it.

KEITH Where?

GERAINT Back lane?

JULIA / KEITH No.

JULIA Bedroom?

GERAINT /
KEITH No.

JULIA Where then?

GERAINT I know.

JULIA / KEITH Where?

GERAINT The Giant's garden.

JULIA He's still away on holiday.

KEITH But we're not allowed.

GERAINT He'll never know.

DAD Geraint!

MUM Julia!

GRANDAD Keith!

GERAINT Come on.

JULIA I do love it there.

KEITH And they'll never know.

GERAINT
JULIA / KEITH Run for it.

They run.

NARRATION

This is spoken as the children discover the garden.

ALL The Giant had a beautiful large lovely garden
With soft green grass
And here and there over that grass stood beautiful
    flowers
Like stars
And there were twelve peach trees
And in the springtime they broke out into delicate
    blossoms of pink and pearl
And in the autumn bore rich fruit
Delicious peaches.
The birds sat on the trees and sang so sweetly
And the children used to stop their games
And listen to the songs.

SONG OF THE BIRDS

Sing a song of springtime
Cos the winter it has been
Sing a song of springtime
And the garden oh so green.

Sing a song of summer
Birds singing in the trees
Sing a song of summer
And the buzzing of the bees

GERAINT   I love this garden.

JULIA   It's so beautiful.

KEITH   Soft green grass.

GERAINT   Glorious peach trees.

JULIA   And beautiful flowers.

KEITH   It's like paradise.

ALL   How happy we are here.

GERAINT   Yes.

JULIA   Really happy.

KEITH   Really

GERAINT   Really

JULIA   Really

ALL   Happy.

GERAINT   I don't want it to ever change.

JULIA   I want to play in this garden for ever.

KEITH   I want to write music in this garden for ever.

JULIA   I want to write poems in this garden for ever.

GERAINT   I want to make things in this garden for ever.

KEITH   For ever.

JULIA   And ever.

GERAINT   And ever.

KEITH   I want to sing

GERAINT   Dance

JULIA   And be happy in this garden

KEITH   For ever

JULIA   And ever

ALL   And ever.

SONG

Say
Sing a song of springtime
All the flowers having fun
Sing a song of summer
All dancing in the sun.

JULIA   I hope the Giant never comes back.

KEITH   I've never ever seen him.

GERAINT   I wonder what he looks like?

JULIA   Where is the Giant?

KEITH   My Grandad says he's on holiday with his friend the Cornish Ogre.

GERAINT   In Cornwall.

JULIA   With an Ogre.

KEITH   I wouldn't go on holiday with an Ogre.

JULIA   But you're not a Giant.

GERAINT   But you look like an Ogre (*Laughs.*)

JULIA   Do you think the Giant will ever come back?

KEITH   My Grandad says he's been on holiday for seven years.

JULIA   Seven years.

GERAINT   (*He counts seven on his fingers.*) That's longer than me.

JULIA   And me.

KEITH   And me.

JULIA   Why is everybody older than us?

KEITH   I do wonder what he looks like.

GERAINT   Let's play Giants, then I can show you.

ALL   Yes.

JULIA   Guess what sort of Giant I am.

She pretends to be a happy Giant – everyone, including the audience, has to guess.

KEITH   Guess what sort of a Giant I am.

He pretends to be a silly Giant. Everyone guesses.

GERAINT   My turn, my turn.
Guess what sort of a Giant I am.

He pretends to be a sad Giant.
Everyone guesses.

JULIA   Here's a poem.
There are Giants that are friendly
There are Giants that are bad
There are Giants that are frightening
And sometimes they are sad.
Watch out for Loud Mouthed Giants
For they can be quite mad
But Selfish Giants, they are the worst
Which is very, very sad.

GERAINT   That's great. Here's a Giant.

GERAINT finds a very big pair of old gardener's wellies. He animates them as puppets as he recites JULIA's poem.

KEITH   And here's some Giant music.

KEITH has set JULIA's poem to music. He sings it, as does JULIA, whilst GERAINT animates the wellies. End of song.

GERAINT   I'm exhausted.

KEITH   That was great fun.

JULIA   How happy we are here.

KEITH   I want to live in this garden for ever.

JULIA   Wouldn't that be fantastic?

KEITH   Let's make music

JULIA   And poems

GERAINT   And things

KEITH   In this garden

JULIA   For ever

KEITH   And ever.

GERAINT /
JULIA / KEITH   And ever.

JULIA / KEITH   We really are happy here.

GERAINT   Remember this bit? (*He makes a noise.*)

KEITH   What's that noise?

JULIA   What?

KEITH   That noise.

JULIA   I don't know.

KEITH   It's getting closer.

JULIA   Could it be?

KEITH   It might.

JULIA   I never did like this bit.

KEITH   Or me.

JULIA   What shall we do?

KEITH   I don't know.

JULIA   It's getting closer.

KEITH   I still don't like this bit.

JULIA   Or me.

KEITH   Help.

JULIA   Quick everybody.

JULIA / KEITH   Hide.

JULIA and KEITH hide with the audience.
The SELFISH GIANT enters, back from his holidays
with a large suitcase. He wears big wellies and looks
like a gardener.

GIANT   What are you doing here in my garden?
My own garden is my own garden
Anyone can understand that
And I will allow nobody to play in it…
but myself.
Now clear off.
All of you.
Out of my garden.
Shoo.
Kids. No respect.
I'd better unpack.

He exits.

JULIA   Guess what kind of a Giant I am.

She pretends to be a SELFISH GIANT. Everyone
guesses.

Yes, a very, very Selfish Giant.

The GIANT returns with a big notice reading
'KEEP OUT – TRESPASSERS WILL BE
PROSECUTED'.

GIANT   Didn't you hear me?
Don't you understand me?
This is my personal property.
My garden.
So clear off.
Keep Out. Cos trespassers will be prosecuted. I
     don't know, you go away on holiday, you turn

your back for seven years and people just take
over your garden as if it's theirs. Not just people,
but children. My beautiful garden. Soon it will
be winter, that'll keep them out.
Just KEEP OUT.

He exits.

JULIA   And so the children were banished from
the garden.

KEITH   For ever.

KEITH / JULIA   How happy we were there.

KEITH   They said.

JULIA   You'll never guess, Mum.

MUM   What?

JULIA   The Giant's returned.

MUM   After all these years.

KEITH   And he won't let us play in his garden
anymore, Grandad.

GRANDAD   I'm not surprised.

GERAINT   And dad, he's put up a big sign saying
keep out.

DAD   I'm not surprised.

DAD / MUM /
GRANDAD   He always was a Selfish Giant.

DAD   Now you can come and help, Geraint.

MUM   And you, Julie, can tidy your room.

GRANDAD   And Keith, run to the shop for me.

DAD / MUM /
GRANDAD   NO EXCUSES!

GERAINT
JULIA / KEITH   Parents!

GERAINT   Let's hide.

JULIA   Where?

KEITH   I don't know.

GERAINT   I do.

JULIA   Where?

GERAINT   In the garden.

KEITH   The Giant's garden.

JULIA   But we're not allowed.

GERAINT   Remember how happy we were there.

KEITH   Well, if we were quiet.

JULIA   Very quiet

KEITH   Perhaps no one would hear us.

JULIA   But what if the Giant catches us?

GERAINT   He won't; not if we are quiet.

KEITH   Very quiet.

JULIA   Very, very, very quiet.

KEITH   I do miss the garden.

GERAINT   And me.

JULIA   And me.

GERAINT   Well

JULIA   Why not?

KEITH   But quietly.

JULIA   Very quietly.

GERAINT   Very, very, very quietly.

SONG

Sing a song of autumn
Fruits falling from the trees

Sing a song of autumn
And the rustling of the leaves.

NARRATION

When the summer was over
And autumn had passed
And the trees had lost their leaves
Winter soon settled in.
With freezing frost and bitterly cold snow and icy
   North winds

SONG

Sing a song of winter
Snow falling everywhere
Sing a song of winter
The trees so tall and bare

*There is a big physical change to the environment.
What was full and glorious now looks empty, cold
and sad.*

NARRATION

But soon it was time for spring.
And when spring arrived all over the land
It forgot to visit the Selfish Giant's garden.
Instead, winter stayed in the garden
The buds did not return
And the trees were still asleep.
Winter spread itself all over the Selfish Giant's
   garden
It seemed
For ever.

GIANT Who's there?
This is private property
My garden.

My own garden.

And I will let nobody play in it.

Now clear off.

All of you.

Out of my garden.

Shoo.

GERAINT /
JULIA / KEITH   Run for it!

They exit.

GIANT   Kids. No respect.

It's so cold, bitterly cold.

Winter, winter, winter

Whatever happened to the spring?

He exits.

There is a definite change in atmosphere at this point. The three elements, FROST, SNOW and THE NORTH WIND are real baddies. They claim the space and are wicked and selfish. This should be a big sequence, a bitter sequence.

Enter FROST, who pulls a large sheet of white fabric behind it like a cloak. The fabric covers part of the garden.

FROST   I am Frost

Freezing Frost

Freezing freezing freezing Frost

I freeze the earth

I freeze the flowers

I freeze the water

Cos I'm Frost

Freezing Frost

Freezing freezing freezing Frost.

Enter SNOW, who pulls a large sheet of white silk behind it like a cloak. The silk covers the rest of the garden.

SNOW   I am Snow.
Cold Snow.
Very very very cold
I cover the earth
I cover the trees
I paint the world white
'Cos I'm snow cold
Bitterly cold
Very very very cold.

Enter THE NORTH WIND wildly with fast streamers that fly through the air.

NORTH WIND   I'm from the North
And I'm wild
I'm wild wild wild North Wind
I blow down trees
I blow down houses
I blow down children
Cos I'm wild
Very wild
Wild wild wild North Wind.

NARRATION

Winter, cold, cold winter
The Selfish Giant's Garden was very cold
And covered in snow
The trees were frozen
It was truly winter.
A beautiful flower put its head out from under the
    snow-covered grass
But when it saw the Keep Out sign

And felt the freezing snow
It slipped back inside the ground again
And returned to warm sleep.
The only ones who were pleased were
Freezing freezing Frost
Bitterly cold Snow
And wild wild wild North Wind.
It seemed that winter would be here for ever
And ever
And ever.

GIANT Oh dear

KEITH sighed the Giant.

GIANT It seems like this winter will be here
for ever and ever. I cannot understand
why the spring is so late in coming.

JULIA He looked out at his cold white Garden.

GIANT I hope there will be a change in the weather soon.
I'm so cold.
Bitterly cold.
Freezing freezing freezing.
Cold cold cold.

KEITH As the Giant sat cold and miserable in his cold,
cold winter garden

JULIA He looked out afar, and could see that spring had
arrived in other people's gardens.

GIANT Why won't spring visit my garden?

KEITH He said.

GIANT I can't understand it.
I just can't understand it.

JULIA I wish we could play in the Giant's garden.

KEITH I'm bored in my bedroom.

JULIA I'm bored in the street.

KEITH You mustn't play in the street, it's dangerous.

GERAINT I miss the flowers.

KEITH The trees

JULIA The birds

GERAINT The space

KEITH The freedom

JULIA The happiness

GERAINT The fun

KEITH The joy

JULIA The laughter

ALL How happy we were there.

JULIA What happened next?

KEITH I don't remember.

GERAINT I do.

GERAINT demonstrates the physical pact.

JULIA Of course.

KEITH How could I forget.

GERAINT Remember this? Look what I've made.

KEITH It's a bird.

JULIA A beautiful bird.

KEITH A beautiful spring bird.

GERAINT It's a Linnet bird. I told you I was busy making
something. I've got an idea.

KEITH / JULIA Tell us.

GERAINT Well.

I've got a bird

You can write poems
You can write music
And we've got big trouble with a Selfish Giant.

KEITH   I don't get it.

JULIA   What's your idea?

GERAINT   Well. You want to make music in the garden.

KEITH   Yes.

GERAINT   And you want to write poems in the garden.

JULIA   Yes.

GERAINT   And I want to make things in the garden. But the
Selfish Giant won't let us.

KEITH / JULIA   So?

GERAINT   What if the Giant wasn't selfish?
What if we could change him?
Then we could play in his garden
And we would be happy.

KEITH / JULIA   But how do we do it?

GERAINT makes the physical pact sign.

JULIA   Of course.

KEITH   How could I forget this bit.   .

They huddle together and share the plan in secret.

JULIA   That's great.

KEITH   Let's do it.

GERAINT   Before it's too late.

JULIA   But we mustn't tell anyone our secret

KEITH /
GERAINT   Agreed.

JULIA   For ever.

KEITH   And ever.

GERAINT   And ever.

JULIA   Including the Giant?

GERAINT   Including the Giant.

They make the physical pact.

Geraint

JULIA   Julia

KEITH   And Keith

ALL   Practised their idea.

GERAINT   They practised

JULIA   And practised

KEITH   And practised.

JULIA   And when they were ready

GERAINT   They went to the Selfish Giant's garden.

During the above dialogue they create the puppet of the LITTLE BOY out of domestic bits and bobs. GERAINT produces a linnet bird that he has been making throughout the play. When the puppet and the bird are fully made the three children make the pact sign.

The children enter the Giant's garden with the Linnet singing the Linnet song.
The bird flies around the garden.

LINNET SONG

Little Linnet
Little Linnet
Flying up so high
Little Linnet

Perfect Linnet
Flying high up in the sky.

Little Linnet
Little Linnet
To the garden you must lead us
Little Linnet
Perfect Linnet
Fly quiet, make no fuss.

Little Linnet
Now Little Linnet
Attract the Giant's eye
Well done Linnet
Perfect Linnet
Quick fly high into the sky.

GIANT   A bird, in my garden,
A beautiful perfect little Linnet
Could this be the beginning of spring at last?

LINNET SONG

JULIA / KEITH   Thank you, thank you
Little Linnet
Your job is nearly done
Thank you, thank you
Perfect Linnet
Now watch and have some fun.

During the last verse Actor 2 has established the LITTLE BOY (puppet) trying to climb the tree. He keeps failing, and starts to cry.

NARRATION

The little boy tried very hard to climb the tree.
The tree was so big
And he was so small

He tried
And tried
And tried
But he could not climb the tree.
And the little boy cried bitterly.

The GIANT sees the child.

GIANT What's the matter little chap?

BOY I want to climb the tree, but I'm too small.

GIANT I can help you.

BOY Can you?

GIANT Yes.

BOY But you're a Selfish Giant.

GIANT Climb on my hand.

BOY Will you squash me?

GIANT No.

BOY Promise?

GIANT I promise.

BOY But should I trust a big Giant?

GIANT Trust me.

BOY Everyone says you're selfish.

GIANT Climb on my hand, trust me.

NARRATION

And the little boy
Climbed into the Selfish Giant's big hand.
The Giant lifted him up
High into the branches of the tree.

GIANT There you are.

NARRATOR The little boy could see for ever.

BOY   I can see for ever and ever.

NARRATOR   and ever
and ever.

NARRATION

The Linnet bird flew around the tree
And as it flew
The snow began to melt
And the frost to disappear.
The winter was over at last in the Selfish Giant's
   garden.
The spring began to bud.
The Linnet continued to sing.
The boy smiled
And smiled
And smiled
And the Giant
Cried.

BOY   Why are you crying?

GIANT   Because you are so happy.

BOY   You are a funny old Giant.

GIANT   If I hadn't been so selfish, the spring would have
come sooner to my garden.

NARRATOR   The little boy smiled.

GIANT   What a wonderful day.

NARRATOR   And as the Giant looked around the garden,
He saw lots of children.
(*Sees audience.*)
He waved at them.
(*Waves.*)
He smiled at them

(*Smiles.*)
He said welcome.

GIANT   Welcome to my garden.
        Welcome, welcome, welcome.
        Please accept my pardon
        Welcome, welcome, welcome
        Welcome all into my garden.

        *JULIA, KEITH and GERAINT make the secret pact
        sign.*

KEITH   It's worked.

JULIA   Our plan has worked.

KEITH   But remember

JULIA   We mustn't tell anyone our secret.

KEITH   For ever

JULIA   And ever.

KEITH / JULIA   Including the Giant.

        They make the pact sign.

NARRATION

The trees were so happy to have the children back
    again
They covered themselves with spring blossom
And waved their arms gently above the children's
    heads.
The flowers looked up through the green, green
    grass
And laughed.
It was a lovely scene.

GIANT'S SONG

Welcome welcome welcome
Please accept my pardon

Welcome welcome welcome
Welcome all into my garden.

GIANT   How selfish I have been
Now I know why the spring would not come here.
From now on, my garden shall be the children's
    playground
For ever and ever.

NARRATION

The Giant reached out his hand to the little boy
The little boy stepped into the Giant's hand.
The Giant smiled.
The little boy smiled.
And the little boy stretched out his two arms and
    flung them round the Giant's neck
And kissed him.

GIANT'S SONG

Welcome welcome welcome
Welcome little friend
Welcome welcome welcome
Much love to you I send.

GIANT   It is your garden now, children.
You can play in it for ever and ever.

He takes down the Keep Out sign.

NARRATION

And as the Giant took down the sign
The cold winter left the garden
And spring had truly arrived.

GIANT'S SONG

Welcome welcome welcome
Welcome short and tall

Welcome welcome welcome
Welcome children, welcome all.

NARRATION

Every day
After school
The children came to play in the garden
With the Giant.

KEITH   Hi Julia.

JULIA   Hi Geraint.

GERAINT   Hi Keith.

KEITH / JULIA
GERAINT   Hi Giant.

KEITH   What shall we play?

JULIA   Let's play chase.

They play a wild game of chase and the GIANT gets exhausted.

GIANT   (*Out of breath.*) Where is your little friend

The children look at each other.

The boy I helped with the tree?

They make the secret pact sign.

JULIA   We don't know.

KEITH   He must have gone away.

GIANT   You must tell him to be sure to come and play tomorrow.

JULIA   But we don't know where he lives.

KEITH   We've never seen him before.

GIANT   How I would like to see him again.

JULIA   You're on it.

They play tag.

NARRATION

Time passed
And the Giant grew old and feeble.
He could not play anymore.

KEITH   What shall we play today?

JULIA   Hide and seek.

GIANT   You play, I'll watch.

KEITH   Are you alright?

GIANT   Just a little tired.

JULIA   You're such a lovely Giant.

GIANT   I have many beautiful flowers in my garden.

KEITH   Yes, there's daisies.

JULIA   Marigolds.

GIANT   Lupins.

JULIA   Cactus.

KEITH   Buttercups.

JULIA   Celendines.

GIANT   Geraniums.

KEITH   Lavenders.

GERAINT   Passion fruits.

JULIA   Poppies.

KEITH   Hundreds

JULIA   And thousands.

GIANT   But you children are the most beautiful flowers of
        all.

KEITH   You're such a kind Giant.

JULIA   Not selfish at all.

GIANT   I wonder what happened to the little boy.
        I do miss him so.

KEITH   Well, you see…

        *JULIA makes the secret pact sign to stop KEITH telling
        the truth.*

DAD   Geraint.

MUM   Julia.

GRANDAD   Keith.

DAD   Tea.

MUM   Tea.

GRANDAD   Tea.

KEITH   Gotta go.

JULIA   Gotta go.

KEITH   See you tomorrow.
        (*Kisses the GIANT.*)
        Bye. (*Exits.*)

JULIA   See you tomorrow.
        (*Kisses the GIANT.*)
        Bye. (*Exits.*)

GIANT   How I would like to see him again.
        He taught me such kindness.

GIANT'S SONG

Welcome welcome welcome
Welcome little friend
Welcome welcome welcome
Much love to you I send.

NARRATION

Time went by
And the Giant grew very old.
And feeble.
He could not play anymore.

JULIA Do you think we should tell him?

GERAINT What?

JULIA That we invented the little boy.

KEITH It was for his own good.

GERAINT And it worked.

JULIA I know, but I think we should tell him why.

GERAINT It's selfish not to, really.

KEITH And perhaps we were being selfish, because we wanted to play in his garden.

JULIA I don't want to make him sad again.

GERAINT Nor me.

KEITH We won't.

GERAINT Look how happy he is now.

JULIA But we must tell him.

KEITH Okay let's tell him.

GERAINT Yes, we'll tell him.

NARRATION

The Giant looked across the garden
He rubbed his eyes in wonder
And looked
And looked
And looked.
It certainly was a marvellous sight.

The GIANT begins to imagine.

In the farthest corner of the garden
Was a tree covered with beautiful white blossom.
Its branches were golden
And silver fruit hung down from them.
And underneath them
He thought he saw
The little boy.

GIANT   (*Imagining.*) How I have missed you.
          It is you who taught me kindness.

NARRATOR He reached his hand toward the little boy.

GIANT   Thanks to you, my garden belongs to the children
          of the world.

NARRATOR But there was nobody there.
          A tear ran down his face

JULIA   We've got something to tell you.

KEITH   It's about the little boy.

JULIA   We were being selfish…

KEITH   We made up the little boy.

JULIA   So that we could come and play in your garden.

KEITH   And stop you being selfish.

JULIA   But we made a promise.

KEITH   Not to tell you.

JULIA / KEITH For ever.

*The GIANT makes the secret pact sign. JULIA and
KEITH look at each other in amazement.*

JULIA   And it worked.

KEITH   But we're sorry.

JULIA / KEITH Very sorry.

The children give the puppet of the LITTLE BOY to the GIANT.

JULIA   It's for you.

KEITH   For ever.

JULIA   And ever.

JULIA / KEITH   And ever.

GIANT   For ever and for ever
Selfishness must pass.
For ever and for ever
A friendship it will last.

GERAINT   I've got to go now and help my dad.

JULIA   I've got to go now and tidy my room for my mum.

KEITH   And I've got to go down the shops for my Grandad.

GERAINT   See you.

JULIA   See you.

KEITH   See you.

They leave.

NARRATION

The next day
When we visited the garden
We couldn't find the Giant anywhere.
We found him
In a corner of the garden
Lying on the floor.
His eyes were closed for ever
And he was clutching the little boy
Close to his heart

Know your flow

The Empowerment Cycle

R

ROCKPOOL

SHARON WOOD

A Rockpool book
PO Box 252
Summer Hill
NSW 2130
Australia

rockpoolpublishing.co
Follow us! f ⓘ rockpoolpublishing
Tag your images with #rockpoolpublishing

ISBN: 9781925946741

Published in 2021, by Rockpool Publishing
Copyright text © Sharon Wood, 2021
Copyright design © Rockpool Publishing, 2021

Design by Sara Lindberg, Rockpool Publishing
Edited by Lisa Macken
Images from creative market and shutterstock

A catalogue record for this
book is available from the
National Library of Australia

Printed and bound in China
10 9 8 7 6 5 4 3 2 1

To a world without
menstrual shame.

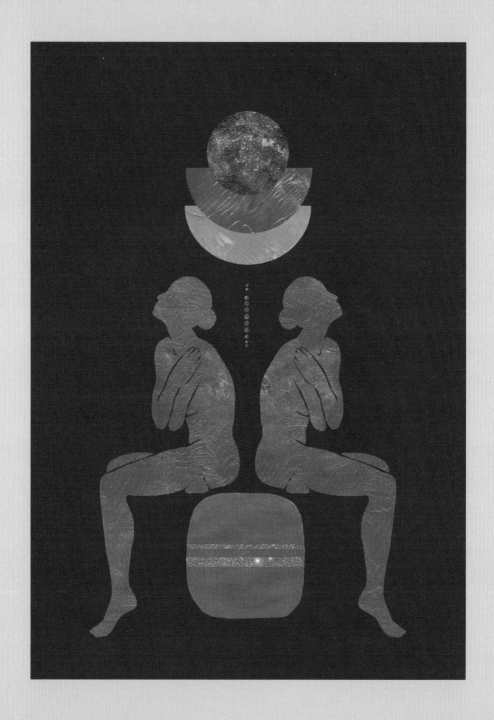

CONTENTS

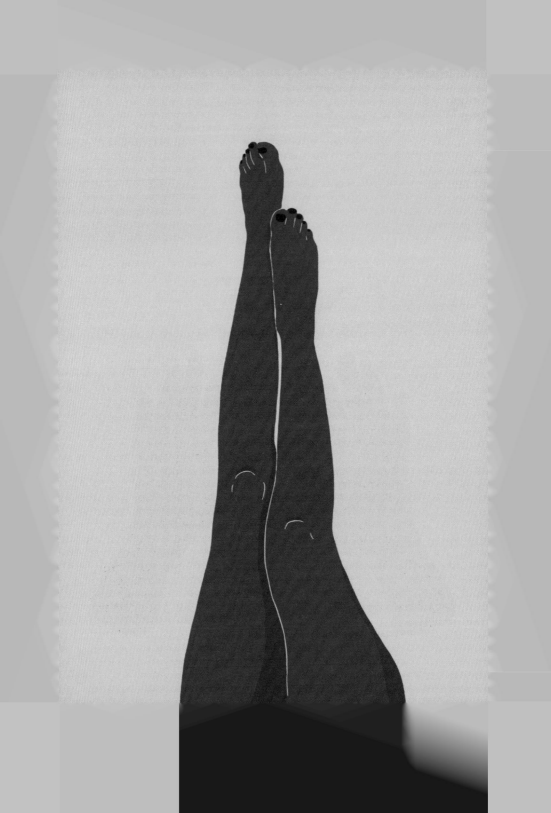

Introduction:
THE BIRTH OF EMGODDESS

᯽᯽᯽᯽᯽ ᯼᯼᯼᯼᯼

'Why am I just hearing about this for the first time?'

It's a rhetorical question I hear constantly when women attend my workshops and learn more about their monthly cycle. This particular time it came from a 53-year-old woman, but the same question has sprung from the lips of young women in their late teens and every age in between. As the founder of Emgoddess, a movement I created in 1996 after discovering the power of the menstrual cycle and how it is connected to so many aspects of women's lives, it has been my mission to shine a light on the one component of being a woman that we are often quick to pretend doesn't exist: menstruation.

But why are we ashamed of menstruation and so prepared to pretend we don't even get a period each and every month? And why am I so passionate about bringing your notice to the lack of attention we give to menstruation? Because it *impacts so* many areas of our lives in the most amazing ways, but many of us haven't come to an understanding of this. At networking events I'd say:

I would come to be known as the 'period lady'

'Hi, I'm Sharon and I wrote a book about periods,' then proceed to do my utmost to spread the word about the work that has been my passion project for the past 24 years. You could literally see the lights in their eyes switch off as they began to dart their eyes around the room, looking for an escape. *Oh, another one bites the dust.* I would be forlorn and then seek out someone else I could spark up a conversation with about the incredible discoveries I was making through Emgoddess.

I get it: it's not the most glamorous topic. To be honest, there was a part of me in those early days that was petrified I would come to be known as the 'period lady', but at the same time I was driven to share the knowledge I'd accrued over years of paying attention to my cycle, of noticing how it had repeating patterns that were unique to me. The more time has passed the more prepared I am to take on the moniker that once made me cringe – anything to reach more women so I can show them how to embrace their cycle and step into their power.

Don't get me wrong: as with any woman, there are many times when I have cursed the fact that I have a period. It has caught me out once or twice and there have been months when the cramps and aches were the final straw for what may have been a rough week. Then I remind myself of how powerful my cycle is, what it allows me to do and how I can tap into the cues my body gives me every single month and harness their power to become my best self – an emgoddess!

The creation of Emgoddess was an accident, as are some of the best things in life. I travelled to the UK with someone I met in my early 20s and began to study natural therapies. One lecturer spoke about women's cycles and the essential oils you can use to help different conditions: 'If you understand your female body, it just makes such a big difference,' she said. She recommended a few different books that would serve as great guides for those who wished to delve deeper, but I never really thought much of it. As a young aromatherapist, massage therapist and herbalism student I ventured into a New

Age-y bookshop and stumbled across two of the titles my lecturer had mentioned. Deciding they had been put in my path for a reason, I bought them both and read them from cover to cover faster than I'd read any books before. Why? I became fascinated, absolutely captivated, by the notion that understanding the way the menstrual cycle works can unlock so much for women.

I began to read more, and the more I read the more I discovered. I started to chart aspects noticed about myself and, through this process, recognised features I liked. I began to pay attention to my cycle, recording my physical and emotional feelings and what was happening in my life in general and how I responded to it. I created my own template and filled it out each and every day, as you would a diary. I was only a few months into the process when I began to see patterns emerging: on certain days in my cycle I would feel sluggish and unmotivated, while on other days I would be flooded with boundless energy and a feeling that I was invincible. Noticing how the patterns appeared around the same time every month meant I could anticipate those days and begin to love my body and my mind.

Discovering Emgoddess and developing the empowerment cycle were major events in my new awareness. Understanding my body has allowed me to build on my times of strength and confidence and support me when I knew I would feel vulnerable and be more susceptible to self-doubt.

I didn't have a lot of connection with my body in my younger years, abusing it fairly regularly with alcohol, crappy food and little exercise. Like many young women I had a personal struggle with low self-esteem and feeling worthless, ashamed and small. It took me many years to find and develop an inner strength that allowed me to stand comfortably in my skin. Starting to chart and focus on myself created that connection, that missing link, which enabled me to stop so I could start recognising all of the good parts of myself. It gave me time to reflect on and acknowledge the positive things that were happening in my life. The ultimate outcome was that it gave me gratitude for my body and who I am: I became *empowered*. Whenever I was feeling upset, angry or frustrated and on the verge of tears, there was also a sense of peacefulness about it, because I knew that in a couple of days I'd be fine again. I didn't go into a downward spiral and head deep down into a rabbit hole; I just had to hold tight and ride the waves of emotion with the knowledge that what I was experiencing was normal.

As I became more confident in my charting and the results it was getting for the women who joined in, I expanded my recordings to include how I dressed, the type of make-up I wore and which activities I gravitated towards, and the patterns occurring in all of these areas began to materialise. Upon completing my aromatherapy course, I began recruiting friends, family and clients of the company I worked for to take up the practice of charting. I was fascinated when women came back to me with their own unique patterns that repeated each month.

How is it that we are not taught this?

It began to puzzle me that the repeating patterns that occur during menstruation are not common knowledge for women, so 20 years ago I set out to change that. I quickly found as I began to introduce my findings to the wider community that the world was not yet ready to hear about it: there was still so much embarrassment around periods and I couldn't get the traction to begin to make real and lasting change in attitudes towards women's cycles. But Emgoddess never truly went dormant. I continued to chart my own patterns, others were on the ride with me and I had gathered hundreds of charts. Out of curiosity I would ask women where they were at in their cycle and explain why I was asking, and they would be very open with me.

We live in a world of menstrual cups and menstrual undies. A lot of women are turning away from mirenas and pills and looking for alternatives to control their menstrual cycle. They want to reconnect with what it means to be a woman. There is a real opportunity for Emgoddess to flourish, and there is a growing legion of women who are embracing this form of empowerment with open arms. Women are more open about their bodies, there is less shame or embarrassment, and they are prepared to break down the stigma that surrounds the messier parts of being a member of the fairer sex.

It's been a slow burn, but my passion has never waned. Pioneers such as Dr Libby Weaver and Ruth Trickey shone the light on the importance of women's hormones, but Emgoddess takes this further by putting the power back into your hands. The empowerment cycle is a combination of charting, self-discovery, mindfulness and discipline: all qualities that will help you to feel stronger, happier and more confident.

After launching my first book, *Emgoddess: Self-discovery guide for women*, in 2016 I was called to link my discoveries with scientific research. As I began to delve into the volumes of validated and peer-reviewed research, I was ecstatic to discover the findings always backed up my intuitive journey in an iron-clad way, which made it imperative to release this new book to solidify the importance of what I have been teaching for decades and to prove this goes way beyond 'woo woo'.

When I first began looking into the research being conducted by professionals in the realm of women and their menstrual cycle, I was stunned: women make up 49.54 per cent of the world's population yet they continue to be embarrassed about their bodies and ashamed of their natural menstrual cycle.[1] A 2018 poll

showed almost 50 per cent of women experienced period shaming at some point in their lives, with one in five being made to feel like the very natural process of menstruating was dirty and indecent because of comments made by a male friend.[2] Even more disturbingly, 12 per cent of the female respondents had been shamed by a family member and one in 10 by a classmate. The same poll, which recorded responses from 1,500 women and 500 men from the USA, found 58 per cent of women felt a sense of embarrassment simply because they had their period.

This may not seem overly consequential, but like a duck that looks calm and appears to glide across the surface of a lake while its webbed feet are busy paddling away just below the surface, these comments and feelings take a toll on women of all ages. The men, family members and school peers who instigate these humiliating feelings with their thoughtless comments simply can't see it.

When you consider that more than 16 per cent of six-year-old girls experience low body self-confidence and 75 per cent of women with low self-esteem engage in negative activities such as cutting, bullying, drug and/or alcohol abuse or disordered eating, it is vital that young girls are taught to love, embrace and celebrate the bodies they have.[3] This is often easier said than done, but it is my hope that as more teenagers and women begin to embody their inner emgoddess their influence will become a beacon of light and a vehicle for change.

Girls will always model the behaviour of the women around them. Showcasing how liberating it is to love yourself, embracing all of the elements of being a woman and channelling the power of the menstrual cycle to assist in all areas of life is one of the first steps you can take to start having a real impact on turning the statistics around.

Research is critical because I want to achieve my goal of turning a worldwide taboo into an empowerment tool. I need to work with young women in schools, sporting and community groups, and evidence-based research is the key to granting me entry into their world to open their minds to the possibility of not only understanding their bodies more but equipping them with the skills to kick ass by harnessing the power of what their bodies do instinctively.

So, I started to look at the research and, more than 200 research articles later, I am *still* finding information that completely supports my charting results and my intuitive findings, among other things. The confirmation has been a revelation for me and for the path Emgoddess has paved since I founded the movement. Knowing there is solidifying evidence out there backing up what I know means I can stand in front of women in my workshops and not just state that these things happen during their cycle, I can also explain *why* from a scientific perspective.

Imagine having a tool that told you: when you have the most energy, enabling you to know your most productive days and that you can smash through a heap of work; when you are most likely to take risks; when you are most influential and able to rally the troops to get shit done; and when you are in the optimum position to assess your life and make changes? **I am sure** if men had access to a tool that told them all of this they would use it to their greatest benefit and not be afraid to show us their super powers! They would endeavour to understand it, perhaps attend courses, and truly utilise this internal tool so they could be better leaders and more successful in their careers or sport.

When you listen to your body through Emgoddess you can discover *today* the power you have. Each day brings with it something positive and potent, and only women have the ability to tap into it. Emgoddess shows you how and identifies the strengths within your cycle, how to look for them and how to use this information to really make the most out of your body.

I discovered there were four distinct phases each month that have an impact on everything: energy levels, mood, physical health, personal interactions and relationships, right down to the clothing you wear and the make-up you use. Have you ever wondered why there are times during each month you feel like you could achieve anything, yet only a handful of days later you are lost and lacking motivation? Why is it that sometimes you can manage with ease all the things the world throws at you, embracing challenges with open arms, while at other times you want to run away and hide or fall into an emotional heap? It is not because you are weak, crazy or incapable of coping; it's because you are in a particular phase of an amazing journey.

Why is it that you can purchase a top and bring it home, pop it on and feel like a runway model wearing it, then a couple of weeks later you put on that same top and feel awful? You haven't changed in size or shape so significantly that you now need to repurchase your entire wardrobe. The only thing that has changed is where you are in your cycle.

The Empowerment Cycle focuses on changing perceptions and attitudes towards your monthly cycle. It teaches you to:

- **embrace** your cycle, your beautiful individuality and your full potential
- **emerge**, recognising the different phases and their appearance in your cycle
- **embody** each of the four phases and create your own rituals each month
- **empower** yourself through heightened self-awareness, treating yourself with respect.

You can use your understanding of Emgoddess to appreciate who you are each day and support yourself through different times of the month. You can plan when to entertain, when to ask for a pay rise and when to start a new exercise regime. An emgoddess truly understands and respects herself. She shows love for herself in what she does and doesn't do. She learns to avoid those activities that bring her down, and she doesn't beat herself up over societal expectations that don't fit her: she accepts and loves herself without judgement.

The more time spent on fostering and nurturing your precious self the more you will shine. Emgoddess promotes self-love and self-respect, which comes from within. Having an understanding of your own body can help you to remain in touch and connected to yourself.

Since launching Emgoddess I have reached thousands of women with my message, and many clients have found it gives them hope. The most rewarding feedback I get from women is hearing that they understand things about their body they had never known before, that they like and love who they are. This is why I do what I do.

CHAPTER 1

Embrace:

UNDERSTANDING THE IMPACTS OF YOUR CYCLE

I n Chinese philosophy and religion everything is divided into yin and yang. I really like this concept when it comes to looking at the menstrual cycle.

The best way to consider yin and yang and their interplay is to look at the cycle of a 24-hour day: in the morning the dark and cool (yin) gives way to the rising sun (yang) and the day starts to warm up. Up until midday yang's warming, drying, moving energies are still building. After that the yang begins to wane as the cooling, darker, damper, nourishing yin energies once again take over. From sundown to midnight is the most yin part of the day, with sunup to midday being the most yang part of the day. Yin and yang are always in transition and transformation; therefore, one cannot exist without the other.

Let's look at this in relation to the menstrual cycle. The first half of the cycle, beginning with menstruation, is related to yin. During this phase the body discharges accumulated blood to make way for the formation of new blood. The blood needs to move downwards smoothly and unimpeded, then towards the end of the bleed the blood and yin begin to build. This ends around ovulation, a time when you perhaps feel more in touch with spiritual matters and have a more feminine energy around you.

At ovulation the yang phase begins. Yang energy is the counterpart of yin. Some Chinese medicine practitioners say this gathering of energy is why pre-menstrual symptoms of painful breasts, headaches, bloating, irritability and anger manifest at this time. As menstruation begins the yin energy reappears. This flow continues through your life, naturally moving from yin to yang.

Most women understand the basics of their menstrual cycle – roughly when to expect it to arrive, its biological purpose and the finer details about what physically happens – but how many women take the time to understand the wide-ranging impacts of their cycle or to tap into the spiritual connection to things such as yin and yang? For every negative thought you have about your period, there are potentially many more positive ones you could have by becoming aware of how your cycle actually supports you in many areas of your life. This book will bust the myth that there are good phases and bad phases in your cycle. There are positives and negatives, light and dark in each phase.

I must admit that while undertaking the research to create this book, wading through verified medical journals and learning from experts in this field, even I discovered new links to our cycles and our thoughts, feelings and physical abilities that I could add to my 20 years of intuitive charting. Things such as our ability to analyse risk, the power our cycle has over addiction in those susceptible to it and also facts about the pain threshold.

Through Emgoddess you'll learn to identify and develop aspects of yourself to boost your sense of self. You will feel more secure, more valued, more positive and more confident in your abilities and decision-making, and more resilient and better able to handle stresses and setbacks. Through listening to your body you'll find it is telling you a lot about how you are feeling and how to cope from day to day. Having an understanding of your own body can help you remain in touch and connected to yourself. Enjoy the process and find the joy in discovering where you are in your cycle and how it affects your daily activity. It only takes a small amount of time to reflect on and chart your day.

It's time to get to know your inner goddesses. No one can tell you how to live your life, but the more time spent in fostering and nurturing your precious self, the more you will shine. Self-love and self-respect come from within.

It's time to get to know your inner goddesses

Young girls in particular are extremely conscious of their changing bodies, and it is while they are young they start to shape views around their bodies and roles. Sadly, many young women frequently report dissatisfaction with their appearance,[4] and many feel that their bodies are not good enough, that they are too fat or thin, their breasts are too large or too small and so on. Young girls are heavily influenced by their mother's attitudes towards body image and reproductive functions, including menstruation. If mums are encouraging and positive then their daughters will share those feelings.

My experience wasn't the best. I'm the baby of five children, and by the time I was getting to menstruation age, my sisters had left the house to live independently. When I got my first period, I remember thinking my world was over; I cried and cried and thought it was the worst thing that could happen to me. I was never told any different and was so embarrassed when I heard my mum on the phone talking to my sisters, telling them I had 'become a woman'. That was it: it was never spoken of again. The impression I was given was that I should just deal with it. Don't get me wrong: my family is loving and caring, but we just didn't talk about this sort of stuff. I really had to navigate through it all myself.

I now have a daughter of my own and I wanted her experience to be vastly different. I stopped shy of doing the menstrual party with vagina cup cakes and red cordial, but I was truly tempted. I wanted her to celebrate the onset of menstruation and appreciate that it was a gift. I know my daughter understands her cycle and that she gets the changes it makes and how it influences so many daily decisions. She knows that when she is having a bad day, she can breathe through it and reassess her situation a few days later. She really does use her cycle as a tool, which is exactly what I want women to do in their lives.

The first step to embracing your cycle is to understand the impacts it has on your daily life beyond needing to have the bathroom cupboard stocked for when Aunt Flow is preparing her next visit! While on this journey of discovery, reflect on how differently you feel about each of the impacts at different times of the month; you may have already pieced together some patterns before you began your official charting. We will take a brief look at the emgoddess phases so you can see how the empowerment cycle's four goddesses work with scientific research to highlight the impacts the menstrual cycle has on women's lives.

THE HISTORY OF MENSTRUATION

Before we set off to make real and lasting change regarding women's perceptions and acceptance of their menstrual cycle it would be beneficial to take time to reflect on how humans considered this natural phenomenon in the past.

Cultures from around the world have different ways of viewing that time of the month, and it's fair to say many of the rituals and expectations of women during menstruation were rarely created to empower and embolden them in any way, shape or form. This unfortunately led to centuries upon centuries of shame surrounding periods that we now need to step up to and abolish.

British historian Greg Jenner looked extensively into how women managed their periods over centuries. He noted that in the pre-antibiotic age, many women suffered from vitamin deficiencies, disease and bodily exhaustion, stressors that wreaked havoc on hormonal balance and caused many more periods in a usual 28-day cycle or for no period to manifest at all. Jenner highlights the first documented cases of women introducing sanitary items into daily life: the 'menstruous rags' mentioned in the Bible.[5] The era between the mediaeval years and the 1800s saw most Western women walking around commando, so belted girdles were introduced to hold linen sanitary towels in place.

Any practices that empowered women with creative energy were seen as intimidating by patriarchal societies, which often viewed menstrual power as unrestrained magic that contaminated everything and was dangerous to men, their way of life and their goods and livestock. It was feared that menstruating women possessed the power to cause a man's death or the loss of his hunting prowess. Thus menstruation changed from being sacred and holy to being unclean and polluting. The menstruating woman was believed to be a source of destructive energy who held within her femininity a tremendous magical power that could not be contained except by shutting her off from the community and the land itself.

At the first sign of bleeding, women were separated from the community, which still occurs in countries such as Nepal, India and Papua. Women are confined to a hut separated from the rest of the village, their only company being other menstruating women. In these cultures it is forbidden for menstruating women to touch the implements of daily life, in particular, anything belonging to a man. In some cultures, the penalty for women breaking this taboo was death.

According to Judaism's Halakha laws a woman is not allowed to touch her husband until she has slept on white sheets for a week, to prove her period has finished. She then has to immerse herself in a sacred Mikvah bath before being allowed to once again sleep in the same bed as her husband. Muslim women are still not allowed inside a Mosque and cannot pray or fast during Ramadan if they are menstruating. Although the tradition of being segregated has long disappeared, negative attitudes towards the menstrual cycle have remained with language such as 'the rags', 'the monthlies', 'the curse' or my particular favourite 'the painters are in . . . they are painting the town red'.

Jenner says that even in mediaeval Europe there was a sense of genuine horror surrounding the monthly blood and women went to great lengths to

mask their cycle from public view, including trying to stem heavy flows with natural remedies such as powdered toad or carrying handmade necklaces of sweet-smelling herbs around their necks to neutralise any odour. Although periods were thought of negatively, the irony was that a woman without a period would not be able to have children.

The modern tampon began its evolution in 1929, and we are now in an era in which we are spoilt for choice with tampons, sanitary pads, panty liners, menstrual cups and period-proof underwear among others.

Psychological factors play a major role in the perception of menstruation and menstrual symptoms, so when educated about the issues, women can make better judgements and openly talk about them with practitioners, friends and family. Through sharing information and asking questions, we can help to normalise menstrual issues and derive a sense of meaning, purpose and belonging. This will have a strong impact on self-perception and emotional well-being.

THE MENSTRUAL CYCLE

The *menstrual cycle* is the name given to the cyclic changes that occur in a woman's body each month generally between the ages of 12 and 55. It is the regular shedding of the endometrium – the lining of the uterus – that occurs every month for most women and makes pregnancy possible. Although menstrual loss looks like blood, it is actually composed of other tissues and secretions from the inside of the uterus.

'Normal' is a silly term for the menstrual cycle, as there is a lot of variation between what a normal period is for women from a range of ages and health and fitness levels. The cycle usually takes 29.5 days – the same length as the lunar cycle – and the shedding lasts for between three and five days. You may find your cycle is much longer or shorter than the norm. I know of women with cycles as short as 21 days and other women with rather long cycles, around 35 days, so only you can determine what your normal is. Contraceptives can influence the natural rhythm, as do pregnancy and menopause. That doesn't mean your inner goddesses have been silenced. You can still chart your cycle, which is explained in Chapter 3.

As it is such an individual thing, it is as important to keep a record of the length of your individual cycle as it is to keep a record on the length of menstruation, the amount of pain experienced and the colour, consistency and amount of menstrual loss.

The menstrual cycle is broken into four stages. I could have nominated celebrities or fairytale princesses for each of the phases, but the stars of today will not necessarily be the stars of the future and fairytale princesses lack the dynamic nature of each phase. I choose to use goddesses as it is easy to explain energies or characteristics through a story or a myth and the stories linked to Greek goddesses are epic. Chapter 2 outlines the intricacies of each of the goddesses and their link to the cycle, but below the physical process of a menstrual cycle is listed, with your first sneak peek at the names of the goddesses allocated to each of the phases.

Stage 1, menstrual phase, days 1-5 (Hecate): the first day of a woman's period is considered to be the first day of the menstrual cycle. If an egg is not fertilised it disintegrates. Levels of the hormones oestrogen and progesterone drop during this phase and cause the lining of the uterus, the endometrium, to break down and be shed in the form of menstrual blood. Bleeding lasts an average of five days. The worst of pre-menstrual syndrome (PMS) is over and some symptoms, especially breakouts, subside.

Stage 2, follicular phase, days 6-13 (Daphne): early in the cycle the pituitary gland in the brain produces rising amounts of follicle-stimulating hormone (FSH), which acts on the ovaries to promote the development of several follicles, each one containing an egg. Only one follicle will reach maturity. Oestrogen levels start to rise as your ovaries gear up a mature egg for ovulation, which increases amounts of the feel-good brain chemicals such as serotonin and dopamine and enhances blood flow to the brain. Toward the end of this phase the ovaries secrete increasing levels of oestrogen, which causes the uterine lining to begin thickening in preparation for a potential fertilised egg.

Stage 3, ovulatory phase, days 14-17 (Demeter): the pituitary gland and hypothalamus release a surge of luteinising hormone (LH) about midway through the cycle, which causes the mature follicle to bulge out from the surface of the ovary and burst, releasing the egg. Ovulation usually occurs around day 14 of the

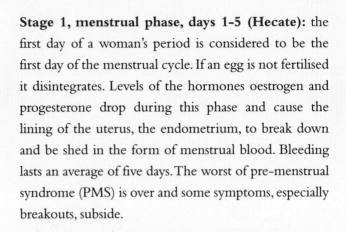

cycle. The egg travels down the fallopian tube and into the uterus, at which time a woman is most likely to become pregnant.

Stage 4, luteal phase, days 18-28 (Persephone): after releasing the egg, the ruptured follicle develops into a structure called the corpus luteum, which secretes increasing amounts of progesterone. Progesterone causes the endometrium to thicken further in preparation of supporting embryonic development. An initial rise in progesterone can cause the skin to produce more oil, making it prone to an outbreak of pimples. As the beginning of the period approaches, progesterone and oestrogen levels drop, causing mood changes and concentration problems.

THE IMPACTS OF YOUR CYCLE

Now that you have an awareness of where each of the phases sits within your cycle we can delve into some of the common and not so expected ways in which your menstrual cycle works to influence things such as your mood, energy levels, the way you see yourself and your susceptibility to risk and addiction each and every day.

Self-esteem, self-image, self-perception, self-worth, self-confidence, self-respect: no matter what words you use to describe it, they all refer to your overall opinion of yourself. When you have healthy self-esteem you feel good about yourself and believe you deserve the respect of others. When you have low self-esteem you put little value on your abilities, opinions and ideas and worry that you aren't good enough. Have you ever thought you're not good enough/pretty enough/slim enough/smart enough? You're definitely not alone, as we live in a society that feeds low self-esteem.

I have struggled with low self-esteem throughout my life, feeling from a young age as though I was the ugliest, dumbest and fattest one in my group of friends. I compensated by being the funniest one, the one who always put herself down in a way that would make others laugh. It felt great to have people smile and want me around, but I found that the more I did this the more I gave others permission to join in even if they didn't want to hurt my feelings. I found myself hearing comments such as: 'You'll do okay, Shaz, but you will never be really successful like some of your other friends are.' And I believed them.

Although common within groups of young women, talk such as this isn't necessary. When I started to understand my body and why I was feeling so differently at the various phases of the month I was able to calm my emotions and steady my nerves from self-doubt.

Our self-esteem is impacted by so many external influences: what we see on social media, negative comments from peers, society's extreme beauty standards and the relationships we have with our friends, parents, siblings and teachers. However, researchers are exploring the idea that the way we feel about our bodies could actually be rooted below the surface, a product of our hormones at work.

As if being a woman isn't hard enough! Studies indicate that adolescent girls are particularly vulnerable to developing negative body image during puberty. A Polish study by researcher Maria Kaczmarek, a professor of biological sciences at Adam Mickiewicz University, and Sylwia Trambacz-Oleszak looked at more than 300 girls aged between 12 and 18 years and their levels of body image dissatisfaction.[6] Their results confirmed a link between body image dissatisfaction and the phases of the menstrual cycle.

What is 'body image dissatisfaction?' The study described it as the 'negative evaluation of body image, when an individual's beliefs about her own actual body size and/or shape does not match how the attributes are judged by others'. Put simply, you see yourself completely differently from how others see you. Kaczmarek and Trambacz-Oleszak found the likelihood of feeling dissatisfied with what you see in the mirror is a whopping 2.4 times higher for girls at their premenstrual phase compared with their peers in the menstrual phase. I know you are probably not surprised to hear this, as it has been well documented that women can experience water retention, negative feelings and food cravings during the premenstrual phase of the cycle.

Early in the cycle, during the follicular phase, women express improved well-being, liveliness, enthusiasm and higher self-esteem and find more pleasure in the little things, which is awesome. This is due to an increased amount of oestrogen, allowing the brain to become more animated and capable of receiving and processing larger amounts of information – and it feels amazing while it

What is 'body image dissatisfaction?'

lasts. Then, four to five days before your period, oestrogen levels drop and progesterone levels increase. The alteration of your nervous cell activity leads to a change in behaviour, with mood swings from angry to frustrated to distressed, a lower libido and even depression. It's no wonder we start to question our self-perception.

Younger women are also often embarrassed or negative about their menstrual cycle and it acts as a catalyst to a negative feeling towards themselves and their bodies. While there are many external causes of low self-esteem that you may not be able to control, embracing the practical value of understanding your cycle could make a big difference.

Women with PMS have lower self-esteem in the premenstrual phase compared with the week following menstruation. A USA-based study conducted by Brock, Rowse and Slade[7] showed a connection between mental health and the menstrual cycle. The researchers compared 278 women at two different phases of their cycle: one group three days before and after menstruation and the other group in the mid-cycle phase. The group surrounding menstruation experienced more feelings of negative self-esteem, anxiety and depression compared with the group near ovulation.

Self-esteem is high during childhood and declines at adolescence, reaching its lifetime low between the ages of 18 and 22.8. Brock, Rowse and Slade's findings show self-esteem often remains low until individuals are in their 50s, when it begins to naturally increase again. I encourage women of all ages to buck the trend! When women have a better understanding of their menstrual cycle and how it impacts their everyday lives, they can embrace a set of skills or tools to combat a range of emotions that can otherwise negatively impact their well-being.

Most women see the majority of their cycle as a non-event and could hardly tell you where they are in their cycle on any given day and move through it without giving it much consideration. However, whenever they are feeling down or stressed it is automatically linked to the menstrual cycle, which paints a picture in many women's minds that having a period is a negative thing, a pain in the proverbial and something that simply needs to be endured. There are so many gifts that you can uncover if you just take the time to listen to your body.

SHAME

Take the time to listen to your body

Although it is a natural process, menstruation continues to be commonly considered an aspect of biology that should not be seen, a topic that should not be discussed. Historically, menstruation was viewed as being dirty or disgusting, and many women feel shame when they are seen with a menstrual product in hand or accidentally bleed through their clothing. The media portrayal of menstruation as a process that needs to be hygienically controlled and the increasing popularity of contraceptives that suppress menstruation exacerbate this problem.

Where did negative attitudes towards menstruation originate? According to a research paper in *Women & Health Journal*, in the late 19th and early 20th centuries members of the American medical profession began to view menstruation and other uniquely female functions as pathological – meaning they are caused by a physical or mental disease. They considered a man's body as normal and women's reproductive functions as signs of their inferiority – harmful assumptions and misconceptions that still persist.

One study suggested that attitudes to menstruation are associated with sexual decision-making and aimed to clarify whether there is a direct link between these characteristics or whether other thoughts, feelings and attitudes are involved.[9] A total of 199 female students from a university in the United States were asked to complete a series of questionnaires in order to assess their:

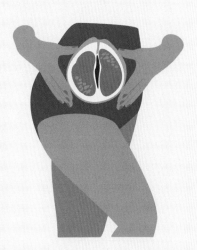

- menstrual attitude
- body shame (negative feelings about the body and desire to hide it)
- sexual assertiveness
- lifetime sexual experience
- sexual risk-taking
- religiosity (how religious they considered themselves to be and how regularly they practised their religion).

The majority of participants were white (67 per cent), with a significant minority of Asian women (19 per cent); were aged between 17 and 23; and nearly all of them identified as heterosexual. The average body mass index (BMI) of participants was 22.7 kg/m2, accurately reflecting the population as a whole, and the average age at which they started menstruation was 12 years.

The results of the questionnaires indicated that roughly half the women had experienced sex and usually with just one partner. The majority (87 per cent) had used contraception the first time they had sex, and a similar proportion used contraception during their most recent sexual activity (88 per cent). There was a clear link between women whose mothers were well educated and lower levels of body shame, and a correlation between Asian women and low levels of sexual experience. In addition, women who were more religious reported that they felt less able to use condoms or other contraceptives when they had sex. Women who had positive attitudes to menstruation and were comfortable with their bodies were more likely to be sexually assertive, use condoms and feel comfortable and confident about their bodies than women with negative attitudes.

The study indicates that menstrual shame is connected to reduced sexual experience and increased sexual risk-taking via body shame and sexual assertiveness. Note that it was a small study and conclusions should be drawn with caution; however, the overall results support the concern that silencing the topic of menstruation may make it difficult for women to feel confident during sex. The study also found a link between being ashamed or embarrassed of periods and general body shame.

Future work should focus on understanding how ethnic background and socio-economic status impact menstrual attitudes, and attitudes among sexual minorities not represented in this study should be investigated. In addition, it is important to explore how menstrual shame might relate to behaviours such as self-esteem, dieting choices and general well-being. Reducing menstrual shame and creating channels for open discussions about menstruation among adolescents may be important for their sexual decision-making as they mature, an important consideration for sexual educators. Promoting positive attitudes towards menstruation could be a starting point in protecting young women from the sexual threats they face. Reproductive shame is common, and research proves women who viewed menstruation as shameful also reported shameful attitudes towards breastfeeding.[10]

A young woman named Rachel who attended one of my workshops grew up in a home in which she didn't ever talk about periods: 'It wasn't the sort of thing I would talk to Mum about; the only thing I "knew" about my menstrual cycle was it "wasn't a good thing".' Over the years Rachel's shame for her cycle expanded to her body image and left her with generally low self-esteem: 'For most of my late teens and early adulthood I found I was embarrassed about my body, and when with a partner I didn't feel confident to say what I really wanted. I put myself in situations I would rather have not have been in. If I thought having more confidence around my cycle would help me as a younger person I would have really liked to know this.'

Hearing stories such as Rachel's is like a red flag to a bull for me and has driven me to remove the shame around menstruation. I urge every woman to know *there is nothing to be ashamed of.* We all experience this monthly phenomenon and I encourage you to think more positively about the miracle of being a woman and what you can now unlock within you to embrace this part of yourself and to empower you to lead a more fulfilling life.

SEXUAL WELL-BEING

Menstrual shame is associated with decreased sexual experience and increased sexual risk-taking. Schooler et. al's 'Cycle of Shame' research piece[11] showed women who reported specific shame about menstruation appeared to be uneasy and reserved about engaging in sexual activity. Not only that, but they also had difficulty with asserting and protecting themselves when they did become involved in sexual encounters. The findings found that silencing the topic of menstruation with a cover of shame made it difficult for women to find their voices when it came to sex in general.

Alternatively, the women in this study who were relatively comfortable with menstruation and their bodies had an absence of shame. This freedom partially accounted for high levels of sexual assertion and low levels of sexual risk reported by these women. Another important finding from the study by Johnston-Robledo et.al[12] concerned sexual promiscuity: women who reported higher levels of shame around menstruation reported higher levels of sexual risk than women with more positive attitudes toward menstruation.

A study published in 2010 in the *Journal of Sex Research* found there was a direct link between the shame women feel surrounding their periods and genitalia in general and the ability to speak up for what they want in the bedroom.[13] Women surveyed for the study who felt shame about their periods reported they were less likely to tell their sexual partners what gave them pleasure. They were even less likely to speak up about the use of condoms or birth control, leading them to engage in risky sexual behaviour. Women who were more comfortable with their periods reported having more satisfying sex and being unafraid to tell partners what they enjoy in the bedroom.

It's important to cover the impact of hormones on your cycles. Specific foods are not relevant for female libido except in how they may temporarily increase testosterone levels. Instead, all of the physiological factors that influence female libido boil down to long-term sex hormone levels and balance. First, absolute levels of hormones are important; for example, the greater the amount of sex hormones in the blood the sexier a woman will feel. Second, balance is crucial; for example, oestrogen is not typically considered important for arousing a woman's sex drive *but* having clinically low oestrogen levels (oestrogen levels below the baseline for proper sexual function) prohibits absolutely any kind of sensation a woman might have in her clitoris. That's scary.

Below is the general effect all hormones have on sex drive.

Testosterone: increases female libido and is the hormone primarily responsible for sex drive in both men and women. When women with hypoactive sexual dysfunction disorder are treated with testosterone they often experienced increased sex drive. Higher testosterone levels also enlarge the clitoris (good to know if yours is shy!) but, unfortunately, if other hormone levels do not rise along with testosterone then symptoms of hyperandrogenism such as facial hair and acne may manifest themselves. Thus testosterone supplementation is not an advisable method of increasing female libido.

Oestrogen: crucial at baseline for sexual function and the primary hormone responsible for vaginal lubrication. However, oestrogen is a testosterone antagonist, so the more oestrogen a woman has in her system the less testosterone she has available to pump up her libido. Therefore, oestrogen dominance is one of the greatest culprits in contemporary Western sexual dysfunction.

Progesterone: another testosterone antagonist. Having elevated progesterone levels relative to the rest of the sex hormones prevents a woman from achieving orgasm.

Prolactin: not talked about very often, since its primary role is in lactation, although it is also involved in pituitary ovary signalling. Rising prolactin levels increase vaginal lubrication and sex drive.

Luteinising hormone (LH): highly correlated with sex drive. LH is a pituitary hormone that triggers ovulation in a woman. Many researchers believe it is one of the primary game makers in sexual arousal.

Because of the role each of these hormones play in female libido, the menstrual cycle demonstrates a clear pattern in fluctuating libido for most women. So how does the menstrual cycle affect female libido? Testosterone levels rise gradually beginning just before menstruation and continue to increase until the next ovulation. During this time frame women's desire for sex has been shown to increase consistently. The 13th day (the cusp of ovulation) is generally the day with the highest testosterone levels and is also the day on which LH spikes.

Ovulation – and no surprise here – is typically the randiest time of the month for a woman. In the week following ovulation testosterone levels are at their lowest and, as a result, women experience less interest in sex. During the week following ovulation progesterone levels increase, which often results in a woman experiencing difficulty achieving orgasm. Although the last days of the menstrual cycle are marked by a constant testosterone level, women's libido may boost as a result of the thickening of the uterine lining, which stimulates nerve endings and makes a woman feel aroused.

Also, oestrogen levels are at their lowest throughout menstruation and into the follicular phase (the first two weeks of the cycle), so women experience the

least vaginal lubrication at this time. However, because testosterone and oestrogen are both increasing, sexual desire is ramping up again in time for ovulation.

SPORT, INJURIES AND PHYSICAL EXERCISE

It's no secret that medical professionals recommend regular exercise to help with menstrual cramps, and weight training is becoming increasingly popular among women as an effective method to control weight and strengthen bones. While some women feel energised during menstruation, others feel more tired, but does the phase of your cycle affect how strong you are, and should you use different workout regimes at different times of the month?

Your training will be impacted by the phases

Your training will be impacted by the phase of the cycle you are in, but not always in a negative way. As discussed, the menstrual cycle is regulated by changes in the four hormones oestrogen, progesterone, follicle-stimulating hormone (FSH) and LH. About one week before menstruation both oestrogen and progesterone levels in the body are at their highest, whereas FSH and LH tend to peak around ovulation at mid-cycle.

Scientists are unclear whether women's muscle strength varies at different phases of the menstrual cycle. The results have been varied, with some researchers reporting women are stronger during ovulation and suggesting that FSH and LH may be involved. Others have failed to find any differences in strength across the menstrual cycle. However, the studies used different measures of strength and only considered the maximum weight women could lift rather than the more recent measure of velocity – that is, how fast different weights can be lifted – to indicate muscle strength and power.

To address this confusion, a recent Spanish study investigated the effects of the menstrual cycle using more up-to-date measures of muscle performance.[14] Thirteen female triathletes with an average age of 31 years volunteered to take part in the study. All the volunteers had regular menstrual cycles, were not using hormonal contraceptives and were familiar with the half-squat resistance-training exercise. The women were asked to perform half-squats with increasing weight up to 80 per cent of their maximum load at three different phases of their menstrual cycle. All trials were performed in a laboratory setting at the same time of day and less than three hours after a meal. The phases of the menstrual cycle were assessed by combining information from a period tracker application, the measurement of body temperature and mass and the levels of LH in the urine.

The study found that neither force, velocity nor muscle strength in the volunteers was affected by the phase of the menstrual cycle, at least not with any statistical significance. This is great news for women, as it means that menstruation doesn't make you physically weaker at lifting weights in the gym or during daily activities.

If you are weight training, it's worth noting this study doesn't rule out the effect of the menstrual cycle on gaining muscle mass. In fact, it seems that the balance of hormones during ovulation increases muscle protein synthesis, so although the muscles have the same strength and power throughout the cycle you're more likely to build up your muscles when you train mid-cycle.

A 2017 study published in the *Journal of Sports Medicine and Physical Fitness* compared the effects of high-frequency resistance training of the legs during different phases of 59 women's periods.[15] All participants experienced benefits from their training, but no matter at which stage of their cycle they trained hardest, it did not affect their growth hormone levels, cortisol levels or bone mineral density. Though neither of the test groups' workout was deemed more effective per se, the group of participants that lifted heavy during the first two weeks of their cycle reported feeling more satisfied with their training.

A compelling reason to train heavy during the week and a half after menstruation is that your body has higher oestrogen levels, which can lead to increased muscular endurance and allow you to hit particular muscle groups harder and more often.[16] This is going to be the time when you'll want to emphasise any sprint and high-intensity interval training work you do because those boosts in endurance can go a long way toward maximising your gains. Women often find that training during their period and right afterwards can help combat negative feelings by increasing a sense of control over their body and musculature.

Associate professor at Melbourne University Adam Bryant said there's a definite link between the female menstrual cycle and lower limb injuries, particularly to the Achilles tendon,[17] because the muscles in the lower leg become more flexible during particular stages of the cycle, such as ovulation, due to the peak in oestrogen and progesterone levels.

Anterior cruciate ligament (ACL) rupture rates are higher at certain points in the cycle; however, more research is needed in this area and other factors such as genetic predisposition are at work. If a player has a history of ACL injuries you may not work on areas such as quick changes of direction in training during phases one and two when you are at a higher risk of injury. You may also have a program of specific preventive or pre-habilitation exercises that lower the risk of this sort of injury. One other thing to watch is the change in your breathing capability, as research shows that the breathing/ventilation rate may increase around ovulation, which is important to note if you are asthmatic.

Everyone's body is different, and there is some great research that shows the benefits of training at different paces at different times of the month. However, do understand that as with everything in your cycle it is very subjective. As you chart more frequently, you'll learn more about training and your body. Just remember to increase exercise levels gradually, listen to your body in terms of how hard you work out and start charting to know where you are in your cycle.

PAIN THRESHOLD

Consider getting a regular deep tissue massage

Dysmenorrhoea is the fancy name given to menstrual cramps, which are caused by the uterus contracting. By

definition it is associated with the menstrual cycle, but the symptoms of several other health conditions can show cyclic variation. This means that the cramping pain you feel can vary depending on where you are in your cycle.

Women are most sensitive to pain in the first half of the follicular phase, during menstruation and a few days after it,[18] due to low levels of oestrogen in the first few days of this phase. There is plenty of research to show a difference in pain level tolerance throughout your cycle. Pain tolerance increases as your oestrogen levels increase and reaches its maximum toward the middle of your cycle, when you will be likely to be able to resume your health and beauty regimen.

To deal with pain, consider getting a regular deep tissue massage. To avoid times of low pain tolerance, you may wish to steer clear of painful procedures around the five days after the end of your period.

BODY TEMPERATURE

It may only fluctuate a small amount, but your body temperature does alter depending on where you are in your cycle.

Basal body temperature (BBT) is the name given to the temperature of your body when it has been resting. Your BBT travels along consistently for the majority of your cycle and, for many, is around 36.4 degrees Celsius. Just prior to ovulation there will be a small dip in temperature, followed by an increase in response to the progesterone that is released after ovulation occurs. An increase in body temperature of 0.3-0.5 degrees Celsius commonly occurs alongside a small increase in heart rate (especially the resting heart rate), which may show for up for you in different ways: you may sweat more or not be able to sustain long efforts as effectively in hot conditions.

Measuring BBT is one of the most common methods used by businesses that help women with their fertility as it can be an accurate indicator of when ovulation has occurred.

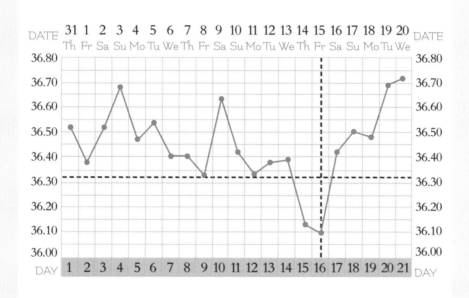

Ever wondered why you wake up brimming with energy one day but then on other days you can't shake off a brain fog no matter how many cups of caffeine you chug?

Your menstrual cycle impacts your energy levels throughout the month, and learning about your empowerment cycle means you can plan your week or month better by syncing high-intensity activities with high-energy days and low-intensity activities with low-energy days. Below is what you can expect from your energy levels in each week of your cycle.

Week 1, slow and steady (day 1 of your period to day 5): the first few days of your period can be a real drain on your energy levels due to the low oestrogen and testosterone levels and the lack of iron from menstruation. Combine this with the pain some women experience through menstrual cramps and you can see why your energy may be low. During this week you may feel tired and withdrawn, so make sure you allow time for rest.

Week 2, take it on (days 6-13): this phase shows a steady increase in oestrogen and testosterone and brings with it a boost of energy. You will be able to speed through tasks more quickly, tackle mentally or physically challenging projects with more ease, stay up late **and** get up early (or pull an all-nighter) and generally push the limits of whatever you want to do. If you have goals to write or a new project to start, this is the time to do it!

Week 3, the great communicator (days 14-17 around ovulation): high levels of oestrogen and a short spike in testosterone will leave you more optimistic, social and motivated this week. This phase brings an ability to communicate with others. Energy levels are up and

steady, and you'll feel great physically and emotionally. Go with it!

Week 4, powerful and passionate (days 18-28, a longer stretch): commonly known as the 'moody cow' phase, this is the phase that gets a bit of a bad reputation. A sudden and steep dip in oestrogen coupled with a rise in progesterone slams the brakes on your energy levels. The first couple of days feel similar to the previous phase, but then the drop comes and you will feel a lot less resilient. These hormonal changes allow you to steady on, making chores and working through a list all good tasks for this phase. You will be highly creative at this time!

SLEEP

For some women the time around menstruation is accompanied by sleep deprivation. In fact, 33 per cent of women say their slumber is negatively affected by their menstrual cycle.

You can blame this lack of shut-eye on fluctuating hormones. Yale Medicine sleep specialist Dr Christine Won says the low levels of progesterone and oestrogen that occur around the start of your period can make it harder for you to fall asleep.[19] During the follicular phase these hormone levels rise, and some women feel drowsy during this phase. Once the egg is released in the luteal phase hormone levels peak, which means sleep may come to you more easily.

We all know the benefits of a good sleep and have experienced the positive feeling that occurs after a

decent number of hours of shut-eye, so make yourself aware of how your sleep alters around your period. If you find that your period interferes with the quantity or quality of your sleep, try following these tips to create your perfect sleep ritual.

Keep a routine: be realistic. I know things change, but if you aim to have a similar time for dinner, rest and bed, it will help you to create a memory association that encourages sleep.

Make tomorrow's to-do list: if you have a busy head you can't switch off, write down everything on your mind and empty your head of all to-do actions that keep you thinking.

Take a hot shower or soak in the bath: the purpose of bedtime routines is to relax and de-stress. On nights when you need extra help loosening up and calming down, a hot shower can work wonders. Use a few drops of your Emgoddess essential oils in bath salts or bath oil and relax.

A long walk: taking a calm, long walk might just do the trick. Walking at a mild pace is relaxing, not taxing, as it helps your mind cool down and your body unwind.

Stretch: find a quiet place and allow yourself to recognise how you feel physically. If you sit in an office chair all day, it's likely that your shoulders, back and legs could use a few minutes of TLC. Stretching also helps you prevent injury and really feel your body, not to mention relieving built-up tension and stress.

Meditate: meditation gives space and perspective to calm racing thoughts that rob you of a good night's sleep. Mastering meditation takes time and patience, and consistency is key; your brain is used to distractions and won't automatically focus and stay mindful in the present. Keep at it, as this mind-calming practice is the perfect way to end your day.

Turn off your devices: we have devices in our hands so much we don't even think about it, but you should really turn off devices in the bedroom. Using TVs, tablets, smart phones, laptops or other electronic devices before bed delays your circadian rhythm (your body's internal clock), suppresses the release of the sleep-inducing hormone melatonin and makes it more difficult to fall asleep.

Use essential oils in a diffuser: diffusing essential oils is a wonderful way to encourage sleep, and there are many essential oils that have a relaxing, calming and even sedative response on the body. If you want to make your own blend try using a few drops of lavender, clary sage, valerian or marjoram in your bedroom at night and drift into a relaxing sleep. Note that essential oils cause a strong response in the limbic brain, the part of the brain that is linked to memory, so if you are using essential oils to encourage sleep, try to only use this combination at night.

SKIN WELL-BEING

Have you ever changed your skincare regime to suit what day you are in your cycle? If your eyes are widening right now your mind is about to be blown: you may be surprised to hear that you can actually get better results with your skin if you change your regime!

Throughout your menstrual cycle, your skin is impacted by the biochemical changes that occur in your body and your skin, being your body's largest organ, is by no means immune to these changes. In fact, your skin is often one of the first ways you can tell that something is off balance in your body. At certain times of the month, you may find your skin becomes drier or more oily or even breaks out. Your body is impacted by what you put into it as much as by what you use on your skin. I always recommend using organic products, pure essential oils and flower extracts to get the best results.

Exactly how each of the four phases can impact your skin health is discussed in more detail in Chapter 2.

FOOD AND NUTRITION

Research conducted by the American Society for Nutrition showed a diet and exercise program that is tailored to counteract food cravings and metabolic changes throughout the menstrual cycle may increase weight loss when compared with women who do not adjust their diet.[20] The study showed how hormones control the menstrual cycle and affect changes in energy intake, expenditure and storage while preparing the body for the possibility of pregnancy every month.

EMOTIONAL WELL-BEING

Taking the time to get to know and understand your cycle can help you to uncover potential links between your hormonal levels and mental health. For example, women with no or few physical symptoms during menstruation are generally not reactive to hormonal fluctuations, whereas women who show many physical symptoms are very reactive to hormonal fluctuations. This reactivity may be general and include both physical and psychological processes.[21]

By tracking and understanding your cycle, you will note the amount of physical effects you are experiencing from your menstrual cycle, which could

help if you are feeling emotions such as depression. The way you feel about yourself and your body will change throughout your cycle: you may find there are phases when you feel confident, self-assured and beautiful and other times when it is a struggle to become motivated to do anything and you feel as though you are in a perpetual fog. Realising that this is what many women experience and tapping into when you are most likely to feel a certain way can help you to move through emotional highs and lows with great confidence.

Creativity is the mental activity that generates novel and practical ideas from pre-existing knowledge, but it may surprise you to learn that intelligence alone isn't enough to make you creative. Interestingly, men and women have different patterns of electrical activity in the brain when they are performing creative tasks, though gender does not affect creative potential overall. These sexual differences in creative brain activity have been attributed to hormones during both foetal development and puberty.

In general, women's brains are wired to give them an advantage in verbal reasoning, detail-oriented tasks and fine motor skills, while men do better at numerical reasoning and visuospatial skills (the ability to mentally manipulate objects). However, research has shown that women's verbal ability is reduced during menstruation while their visuospatial skills improve. At this stage of the menstrual cycle both oestrogen and progesterone hormone levels are relatively low. Oestrogen appears to enhance typically female skills such as verbal reasoning during ovulation, in the middle of the menstrual cycle.[22]

Knowing that different types of creativity are enhanced at particular phases of the cycle or that menopause or hormone replacement therapy could affect them is hugely empowering to women, as it provides a better understanding of when you might be better at reading maps or at creative writing, for example.

A 2013 research study analysed the creative abilities of 28 women and 10 men to identify gender-related differences and the effect of the menstrual cycle in women. Participants were all 18 to 25 years of age and had similar IQs. Tasks were provided to test four aspects of creative thinking: fluidity (the volume of ideas generated), flexibility (the value of the ideas), originality (the novelty of ideas) and elaboration (the depth of the ideas). The results found that verbal creativity was lower

during menstruation, suggesting that some forms of creativity do vary during the menstrual cycle.

The participants in a different study were given a verbal memory task such as remembering a list of words, as well as a virtual navigation task such as finding their way through a maze in a video game that could be solved in several ways.[23] At the end of the experiment, participants were debriefed on how they solved the tasks from beginning to end. The results were clear: women who were ovulating performed better on the verbal memory task, while women tested in their pre-menstrual phase were better at solving spatial navigation tasks.

This proves that women tend to use different strategies to solve tasks depending on where they are in their menstrual cycle. Essentially, the study shows the hormonal changes women experience throughout their cycles have a broader impact than previously believed and have significant effects on how women approach and solve problems.

Clearly, more research into how the menstrual cycle affects creativity would be beneficial, but you can learn more about how it affects you by charting your cycle to uncover where your strengths are within each month. You can then use this information to plan ahead and ensure you are making the most beneficial decisions and tapping into the best parts of yourself each and every day.

RISK APPETITE

You may be fascinated to know how the impact of where you are in your cycle can affect your attitudes towards risk and loss in financial decision-making. Previously outlined was how the different levels of hormones such as oestrogen and progesterone in the body can impact mood, reasoning and thinking, and now a Canadian study has shown how hormonal levels may impact your attitude to spending![24]

Oestrogen and progesterone receptors are present in the nucleus accumbens, a key region in the reward-processing and decision-making part of your brain. Since changes in brain activity related to reward and emotional processing are seen across the menstrual cycle, you might expect economic choice behaviour to be affected by the changing levels of oestrogen and progesterone across the menstrual phase.

There is evidence that hormone levels at the time of ovulation may influence decisions including sexual and mating preferences and traits in mates, as well as clothing styles. The Canadian study looked at three things: rationality, risk tolerance and loss aversion. It showed women were slightly less risk adverse during ovulation than at other times of the month, so a bit more likely to take a risk then. It may be that women take risks during this high fertility phase in order to increase the probability of attracting a partner. Women took significantly more gambles and were less bothered about loss during ovulation than they were during the other phases. The research findings showed that where you are in your cycle phase *does* matter in your choice of behaviour.

The first topic of irrationality was a bit of a surprise for me. As much as we want to say we feel irrational at different times of the month, most commonly in the premenstrual phase, this study showed no evidence women act irrationally at different times in their cycle; their behaviour was always logically consistent. Risk aversion didn't vary significantly; however, women were slightly less risk adverse during ovulation than at other times of the month. The study found the most significant change was around loss aversion, or the tendency to prefer avoiding losses as opposed to getting equivalent gains. Put simply, 'It is better to not lose $5 than it is to find $5.' Women took significantly more gambles and were less bothered about loss during ovulation than they were during other phases.

The findings of the study showed that where you are in your cycle phase *does* matter in choice behaviour, although never in an irrational way.

OUTWARD EXPRESSION

What activities are you drawn to at different times in your cycle? Are you more interested in going out and playing sport or staying at home baking or reading a good book? What is your confidence like? Are you really organised and focused at different phases of the month, and do you feel like this more than once in the month? Look at how others around you affect your thoughts and feelings.

Clothing is a great aspect of your cycle to observe as it's a key indicator of mood. Studies have shown that different phases of the cycle influence changes including how you dress, how you walk and the mates your prefer.[25] You may have a cupboard **full** of clothing yet on some days you can stand in front of it and **swear** you have **nothing** to wear, or you pop on an outfit that makes you feel spectacular one week and makes you cry the next week. When you stop and think about it nothing has changed: you haven't put on 10 kilos, you haven't altered your hairstyle or grown an extra arm. The **only** thing that is different is where you are in your cycle.

Your clothing choices – anything from what you wear on the outside to your underwear, the jewellery

Clothing is a great aspect of your cycle to observe

adorning your body, your choice of make-up and the fragrance you dab behind your ear – can make you aware of where you are in your cycle and allow you to enjoy and play within your goddess energies. Your clothing, hairstyles, make-up and jewellery choices reflect and express these energies in image, colour and shape. Altering your clothing throughout your cycle reinforces the qualities of each phase within you.

The benefits of using your clothing to express the energetic phases are a way to:

- cut yourself some slack and avoid giving yourself so much grief when you have nothing to wear or it doesn't fall just so
- dress in accordance with your energy level
- outwardly express your inner desires and impulses
- enjoy and explore your wardrobe, making the most of your purchases
- have fun with accessories and shoes

Women dress more provocatively when ovulating, a behaviour found to be especially pronounced in those single ladies who are actively seeking romantic partners.[26] Hopefully, now that you know this you won't throw out your entire wardrobe because you can't find anything to wear! It will give you an understanding of how you are feeling in your own skin so you can support yourself better and build stronger self-confidence and self-esteem.

SCENT

At different times of the month, you may be drawn to different aromas: during particular phases you may be attracted to more earthy scents, whereas in other phases you may like the sweet freshness of lighter fragrances. It is amazing how your preferences change. Many studies have shown how our own scent changes and is identified by members of the opposite sex. Pheromones are chemical substances that serve as a stimulus to other individuals of the same species for one or more behavioural responses, which in humans has most often been linked to physical attraction.

In one study[27] body odours and secretions were collected from different parts of women's bodies at various times throughout their menstrual cycles then presented to the women's partners to rank in order of preference. It was discovered across the board that odours collected during the ovulatory phase were deemed to be more pleasant.

There are several components to odour in the ovulatory phase, including steroid hormones from apocrine sweat glands, which signal peak fertility and are favoured regardless of reproductive intention.[28]

Week 1, menstruation: starting from the first day of your period through to day seven in your cycle your oestrogen levels are at their lowest but rise day by day. Your sense of smell starts off fairly low and increases through the week, meaning you're fairly indifferent to scent throughout this week.

Week 2, follicular phase: oestrogen peaks during the second week of your cycle, as does your sense of smell.

This doesn't necessarily mean you'll despise all smells – in fact, it could be a week in which your heightened senses mean you love certain fragrances – but because you'll be picking up on fragrance notes that you might usually miss, it could mean you dislike fragrances you usually tend to enjoy.

Week 3, follicular phase: during the third week of your cycle, oestrogen levels slowly start to drop off while progesterone and testosterone rise. Interestingly, some researchers believe that we tend to crave fatty foods around this time of the month as our sense of smell is heightened to specifically pick up kilojoule-dense food in order to prepare our bodies for pregnancy. Humans *are* clever.

Week 4, luteal phase: during the last week of your cycle your oestrogen levels plummet, which is why you can often get easily annoyed. This irritability is often spiked by heightened senses in general to loud noises, unpleasant tastes and so on, therefore if you smell a strong scent during this time you might be more likely to feel overpowered by it and dislike it.

ADDICTION

Drinking was a big thing for me for many years of my life. I tried to stop but always returned to alcohol within a few months. When I finally made the bold move to quit alcohol forever it was because I had taken notice of a few signs that showed me my drinking was getting out of control. I completed a quiz and realised I was consuming on average around 55 units of alcohol a week! Alcohol impacted my life hugely: I changed jobs and roles at places I really have loved and I was overlooked for opportunities as I looked like I had too much on. Truthfully, though, it was the alcohol that was holding me back.

How did I make the change? I wanted to use my cycle to support me through this huge challenge as I knew it impacted my life. I downloaded some of my charts, popped them in a folder beside my bed and started to chart with a slightly different focus.

In the first month of charting, I really focused on how I was feeling. I charted when I was craving a drink and when I wanted sugar or chocolate instead. I charted my emotions, the days I was feeling amazing and positive, frustrated and moody as well as the days I was a downright bitch about it. In the second month, I continued to chart this information, but I really started to listen to my body and energy levels. I noticed immediately when I woke up feeling great and mornings when I didn't feel that crash hot.

Giving up an addictive substance is much more than simply stopping. You have times when your body fights the decision and you wonder why you are stopping at all. I found this was strongly influenced by where I was in my cycle.

By month three I could see the patterns. I was feeling great during days five to 10 and didn't really

Women can have different responses to addiction

need the booze. I was strong and determined and focusing on things I really wanted to get done. I noticed an increase in my cravings around ovulation (days 12 to 14), a time when the body is feeling spectacular and is looking for a bit of a reward. Days 18 to 27 were when I particularly noticed how charting was helping me: I had days when I was cool, calm and collected and days when I could smash down a litre bottle of chardy. Charting supported me in a way I truly never thought possible, as it allowed me to record my thoughts, process how I was feeling and prepare myself for what I knew was coming each day.

After years of sobriety, I can honestly say I don't think I will ever drink again. I am treating myself with love and respect and my family, friends and I are all reaping the benefits. I am more confident, effective and positive and less anxious, and a few physical changes have helped: better skin and brighter eyes and I've dropped a dress size.

There is growing evidence about how women can have different responses to addiction; the changes in hormones throughout the month can stimulate areas of the brain responsible for cravings and desire. Women have a higher risk of relapse in the late follicular phase of their cycle, when oestrogen levels are higher (around day 10 to 14).[29] This links with research showing how the high levels of oestrogen also activate the rewards centre of the brain, increasing the cravings for the addiction.

One study looked at female smokers who tried to quit.[30] Smokers in the second part of their cycle (the luteal phase, when progesterone levels are higher) found it easier to give up compared with the second group, who were all in the first part of their cycle (the follicular phase, when progesterone levels are lower).

The reward centre of the brain is much more attuned to the pleasurable effects of alcohol when oestrogen levels are elevated, according to a study on mice at the University of Illinois in Chicago.[31] Researchers found that neurons of the brain called the ventral tegmental area (also known as the reward centre), fired most rapidly in response to alcohol when their oestrogen levels were high.[32] This means women experience a rise in oestrogen around day 12 of their cycle and then another, smaller rise around day 20 to 22. As you move to the luteal phase of your cycle both premenstrual and withdrawal symptoms intensify.

Although women are less likely to suffer from alcoholism and consume less alcohol in general, the gap between men and women is decreasing. Young women in particular are far more likely to have indulged in binge drinking during their lifetime than have older women. Studies have also shown that women progress from moderate drinking to alcoholism more rapidly than men, which raises the question: is the menstrual cycle responsible for this difference?[33]

There are two ways in which the menstrual cycle could have an effect on women's alcohol consumption. First, hormones could modify the body's ability to metabolise alcohol, but research has so far failed to support this theory. Second, hormones could change the extent to which alcohol affects women's behaviour, and a few small studies have hinted at this possibility.

Women are more likely to feel depressed, tense and anxious in the luteal phase, the phase typically associated with premenstrual syndrome (PMS).

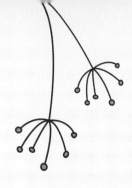

Conversely, women are more likely to feel vigorous, aroused and friendly during the follicular phase. The phase of the menstrual cycle has no effect on the ability of women to perform tasks, apart from balancing. Balance was significantly worse after alcohol in the luteal phase compared to the follicular phase, but women with a family history of alcoholism recovered from this effect more quickly.

The findings from various studies highlight the importance of getting treatment for severe premenstrual symptoms or using natural methods to alleviate them. If you have a family history of alcoholism or feel that you may have an alcohol problem, you should be particularly vigilant during the week before menstruation, when you are more likely to turn to alcohol because of your mood. Although many women feel that alcohol makes them feel better at this time it often worsens their depression.

Recent figures show that 35 million people worldwide suffer from drug-use disorders, and only one in seven receive treatment.[34] Apart from the risk of death from an overdose, drug abuse has a significant effect on physical and mental health in general. According to the United Nations Office of Drugs and Crime alcohol-use disorders are even more common, affecting around 1.4 per cent of the global population (107 million people).

Drug addiction and alcoholism are diseases that affect the mind and body of the user, influencing their feelings and behaviour. They can destroy families and relationships, removing the support so desperately needed by sufferers. Addiction is characterised by the high probability of taking a drug or a drink while trying not to. The phenomenon of increasing desire for something while abstaining from it is termed 'incubation of craving'.

One of the biochemical causes of addiction is the hormone and neurotransmitter dopamine. Dopamine release is important for learned associations, for example, between feelings of pleasure and drug use. These neural pathways encourage drug use and can be triggered by stressful events or exposure to an environment in which the drug was previously used – for example, a pub or a drug-using friend.

Historically, men have been more likely to use drugs, which means that research into addiction has focused on men. However, alcoholism has become far more common among women in recent decades and teenage girls are now experimenting with marijuana, alcohol and cigarettes at higher rates than boys in the US, so research is beginning to be conducted on addiction among women.[35] The studies have found that women are more likely than men to escalate from occasional to heavy drug use and are quicker to succumb to the associated social and physical damage. Women experience higher levels of craving during abstinence, and are more likely to relapse in response to stressful events or a depressed mood.[36]

Oestrogen and progesterone levels fluctuate during the menstrual cycle. Progesterone appears to reduce oestrogen's effect on cravings, with one study showing that boosting progesterone levels in women can reduce the pleasure they get from drugs, which suggests progesterone could be used to treat addiction in women and investigations into this possibility are already underway. Alternatively, artificially lowering oestrogen levels may reduce cravings and could potentially be used to treat addiction. Removing the ovaries of rats so that they cannot produce oestrogen reduces their apparent desire for stimulants; and adding oestrogen back into their bloodstream brings the cravings back again.

In the absence of hormone manipulation, paying closer attention to their menstrual cycle could help women to fight addictions. In 2008, a doctor tested this theory by asking a group of female smokers to try to quit either during the luteal phase of their cycle, when progesterone is dominant, or during the follicular phase, when oestrogen is dominant. Considerably more women in the luteal group managed to quit smoking (34 per cent) than in the follicular group (14 per cent).

Managing hormone levels through the use of oral contraceptives can be effective in balancing mood swings for many women, which could potentially improve the chances of overcoming addiction. However, not all women respond in the same way to oral contraceptives, and further studies are needed before this treatment is recommended to women at risk of relapse.

In general, keeping an eye on your menstrual phase could be useful if you are recovering from addiction. You should be particularly vigilant in recognising cravings around the follicular phase of your cycle, as during these two weeks prior to menstruation oestrogen levels exceed those of progesterone and are likely to create a stronger desire for addictive substances.

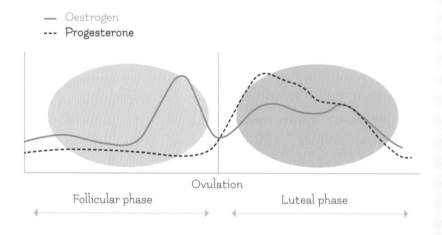

I'd just like to take an aside here to discuss the idea of 'syncing': from sharing tampons, heat packs and paracetamol to accompanying each other to the supermarket for that chocolate fix, there's no better bonding experience than being 'synced up with your best friend. Alone you might feel bloated, tired and grumpy, but together you're powerful force of femininity embracing your inner goddesses. Right?

The idea that women's menstrual cycles can sync up with those they spend the most time with has been around for centuries: a whopping 80 per cent of us believe our periods synchronise with the women around us.[37] While the myth has been around for hundreds of years, the phenomenon was first examined in a research setting in 1971 via a study of female college students conducted by Martha McClintock.[38] McClintock's study concluded that there is a correlation between matched cycles and the amount of time spent with other women, and it's all down to the pheromones that are produced.

80 per cent of us believe our periods synchronise

While you will find many arguments backing the idea of menstrual synchrony, academics such as McClintock have been criticised for poor research methods and a lack of hard evidence. Frederick Naftolin, professor of obstetrics and gynaecology and chairman of reproductive biology research at New York University, says we will never be able to find a definitive answer to the science or existence of syncing.[39]

Any woman's emgoddess chart will clearly indicate that every woman has a unique cycle. Some women have a three-day period while others may have to wait out a whole ten days! It is thus very unlikely that two women's cycles could actually meet up for more than a couple of months at a time – unless, of course, they are using the contraceptive pill.

CHAPTER 2

Emerge: THE FOUR PHASES OF THE MENSTRUAL CYCLE

❧❧❧❧❧ ❦❦❦❦❦❦

Almost every culture throughout history has represented womanhood from adolescence through to menopause in four stages. I use four phases of womanhood to represent the energies you move through each and every month. Their influence may be subtle, but they affect the way in which you go about your day-to-day life. During the phases of your cycle you may be aware of just a few recurring feelings or emotions, yet as your cycle progresses you are thrust into a situation that calls forth another goddess phase.

I named the phases after Greek goddesses who displayed the character traits we embody during particular times in our cycles, and to allow us to celebrate ourselves as divine beings: Hecate, Daphne, Demeter and Persephone. They symbolise your playfulness, humour and irony intermingled with the seriousness of womanhood. Understanding the goddesses will help you to fathom the depth of your own mystery.

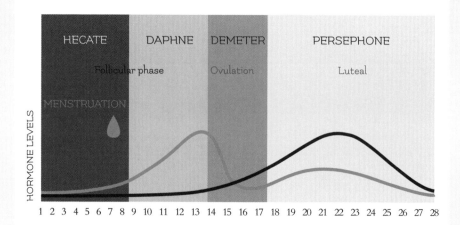

Hormone changes in an average cycle

HECATE   DAPHNE   DEMETER   PERSEPHONE

Follicular phase   Ovulation   Luteal

MENSTRUATION

HORMONE LEVELS

1 2 3 4 5 6 7 8 9 10 11 12 13 14 15 16 17 18 19 20 21 22 23 24 25 26 27 28

E2 (Estrogen/Estradol)
PG (Progesterone)

Explore yourself in terms of these archetypes: let yourself shine like Persephone and Daphne, feel the maternal love of Demeter or embody Hecate, a complete and content woman. These goddesses manifest in each of us, so let's acknowledge and have fun with their characteristics in our everyday life. Once you learn the intricacies of each of the phases you can begin to let your inner emgoddess emerge and begin to embrace the beauty of womanhood.

Embrace the beauty of womanhood

A young, beautiful nymph, Daphne was a huntress and delighted in woodland sports and the spoils of the chase. Many lovers sought her, but she spurned them all and asked her father if she could always remain unmarried. When Apollo first saw Daphne he saw her eyes as being bright as stars. He admired her hands and arms, naked to the shoulder, and whatever was hidden from view he imagined to be even more beautiful. When Apollo came looking for Daphne she became frightened and prayed to her father for help; he told her that he would turn her into a laurel tree to protect her. A stiffness seized all her limbs; her bosom was enclosed in a tender bark; her hair became leaves and her arms became branches; her foot stuck fast in the ground as a root; and her face became a treetop, retaining nothing of her former self but her beauty.

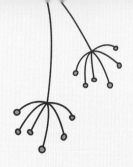

Apollo stood amazed. He touched the stem and felt the flesh tremble under the new bark. He lavished kisses on the wood and embraced the branches, which shrank from his touch. Since Apollo could no longer take Daphne for his wife he made her *his* tree, to be worn as a crown and adorn his harp and arrow. The Daphne phase is most commonly from the end of menstrual bleeding to the start of ovulation. Like Daphne, this phase is one of enthusiasm, confidence and renewed energy as Daphne is pure joy to have around. People love her energy, positivity and vitality and are drawn to her. However, Daphne is as happy in the company of friends as she is by herself, as this phase is quite independent.

The energies of spring are mimicked in this phase, a time of renewal and inspiration. Your inner Daphne has boundless energy and requires less sleep: you are stronger mentally, physically and emotionally, confident and determined and your thinking is clear and focused. In the Daphne phase you will generally feel lighter both physically and emotionally.

RELATIONSHIPS AND SEX

You can come across as a little cold and partners can find you somewhat intimidating due to your self-confidence. You are quick thinking at this time and have a sharper wit and sometimes sharper tongue. If you are in a relationship you may have renewed excitement towards it, finding it exciting and happy rather than clingy or smothering.

The emphasis of this phase is on fun and flirting rather than overt seduction. Sensuality is new and fun

loving and can be expressed it in your hairstyle, clothing and jewellery. With her positive attitude, Daphne is always great fun at a party, and she will help others to defend any unjust acts.

PHYSICAL WELL-BEING

At the onset of menstruation, your pituitary gland releases a hormone called follicle-stimulating hormone (FSH) in response to the drop in progesterone and oestrogen during menstruation. FSH stimulates growth of a follicle (egg) in the ovaries. As the egg grows, it starts to produce oestrogen. Once the egg has matured around day 13 the pituitary gland releases a surge of luteinising hormone (LH), which causes the follicle to rupture and the egg to be released from the ovary.

As oestrogen steadily inclines so do your mood, energy and concentration levels. This increases amounts of the feel-good brain chemicals such as serotonin and dopamine and enhances blood flow to the brain. Toward the end of this phase the ovaries secrete increasing levels of oestrogen, which causes the uterine lining to begin thickening in preparation for a potential fertilised egg.

Cleansed, light and energetic; full of energy and feeling physically great! All the bloating and swelling has gone and you will feel ready for the next phase.

SPORT, INJURIES AND PHYSICAL EXERCISE

A study conducted by researchers at Canada's University of British Columbia found that female swimmers' fastest times occur on the eighth day of their cycle, with

slower results at the premenstrual phase.[40] This study also mentioned that cross-country skiers had their best times just after ovulation and just after menstruation, so in the follicular phase and early luteal phase of the cycle. This is possibly because oestrogen helps muscles better absorb glucose, a sugar in the blood that provides your body with fuel.

This is a time when you may wish to push hard in training due to higher energy levels, and research has shown that muscle tissue repair is increased here, which can help you to recover quickly from intense sessions. Make sure you give yourself time to rest and repair: as you can feel so good during this phase you may not give your body enough time between trainings. Research in 2017[41] revealed the surprising statistic that women are three to six times more likely than men to suffer musculoskeletal injuries in the later stage of the follicular phase closer to ovulation, when oestrogen levels are high due to increased joint laxity. Thus, it's important to warm up appropriately and be aware of overtraining, especially during sessions where you may be doing a lot of sharp direction changes.

SKIN

Increased oestrogen levels can reduce sebum secretions and stimulate collagen production; therefore, you will be less prone to breakouts and will have the best skin. It is a great time to try new skincare products, exfoliate and use a mask.

A reduction in sebum secretion can mean your skin feels a little on the dry side, so ensure you moisturise.

FOOD AND NUTRITION

As this phase follows your period, you need some serious nutrients. Replenish iron stores and eat nutrient- and protein-rich foods to support a healthy uterine lining and a healthy egg in preparation for ovulation. Blood sugar levels are more stable in this phase and therefore you may experience a decrease in appetite.

Your body can metabolise carbohydrates more easily as it is more insulin sensitive; whole grains to get into your diet include quinoa, buckwheat and brown rice. Starchy vegetables including parsnip, sweet potato, pumpkin, green beans and corn will also be beneficial at this time, as will an increase in vitamin C–rich foods.

BENEFICIAL FOOD	Asparagus, pumpkin, sweet potato, peas, figs, lemon
TO CURE THE CRAVING	Vegetable chips, dates, popcorn, peanut butter
AVOID	Refined sugar and alcohol
ESSENTIALS	B vitamins, iron, magnesium, collagen-building foods, vitamin C

RISK APPETITE

During the early stages of the follicular phase of Daphne, women are more loss adverse and thus take less risks.

EMOTIONS AND MOODS

This phase is one in which you will feel self-confident, positive, independent and inspired. Daphne doesn't have time for negative people or people who are holding her back.

You will be happy to be around others as you are great company. Others will want to be around you and you will enjoy the company of others. You have the self-awareness to know what will be the better option for each day. Your confidence will be boosted and you will be mentally, physically and emotionally stronger. This phase brings with it clearer thinking and a focus on the tasks ahead.

Because of the new energy and vitality of this phase, it is an excellent time to take on new projects. Sit and write out your goals such as the pay rise you were wanting. Daphne really feels she can achieve anything, so you'll become clearer about where you really want to be and the things you enjoy in life.

ALCOHOL

This is a phase in which you may find a lack of interest in drinking. Cravings will be low and your focus elsewhere.

SLEEP AND DREAMS

Sleep improves in this phase as your body is using energy. If you are taking up the excess vitality you feel in this phase, it is a great time to ensure you are giving your body the rest it needs to repair and restore.

CONCENTRATION AND CREATIVITY

You may be much more disciplined and focused, so this is a great time to get things done. Take advantage of and enjoy your clear-headed state.

It may be a good time to begin a fresh project, as your current feelings of independence will allow you to take on things you may not normally be confident enough to tackle. Use your clear thinking to draw on your strengths to complete tasks. This is a great time to do more of everything: exercise, socialise and manage projects; nothing can fail.

CLOTHING AND MAKE-UP

Being the beginning of a new cycle means you are not suffering from any bloating from fluid that may arrive toward the end of each month. You may be ditching your old comfy clothes and opting for tighter, firmer fitting clothing.

Make-up will tend to be fresh and light: a touch of gloss lipstick and perhaps some glitter – anything to make you feel great about yourself! Sensuality is new and fun loving, so express it in your hairstyle, clothing and jewellery. Daphne is more likely to wear younger styles of clothing: virgin white or pretty pastel colours.

As you may be more inclined to exercise or get out and about generally, you could be drawn to trousers or jeans matched with a sporty pair of sneakers, allowing movement and flexibility. You may like to wear girly styles and have clips in your hair. The Daphne phase may see you gravitate toward white cotton underwear with pretty floral embroidery.

CHAKRAS

The chakras most aligned with this phase are the sacral and solar plexus chakras. The sacral chakra, svadhishthana, concerns lessons about sexuality, work and physical desire. This chakra is about self-confidence and self-respect and enhances passion, creativity and joy. The solar plexus chakra, manipura, concerns lessons about ego, personality and self-esteem and is also linked to self-confidence.

COLOURS

Colours at this time will represent energy and fun, such as yellow and orange. Orange, which is linked with the sacral chakra, is a beautifully radiant colour full of energy and joy; think about when the sun is shining. Orange inspires creative ideas and a love of life. Yellow is the colour of the sun above us and is happy and full. Dispersing all fears, yellow gives you the confidence to take on the world.

OILS

You will be most attracted to fresh, citrusy scents with a little spice to get things moving in this phase.

GINGER (*Zingiber officinale*)	Ginger helps to create self-awareness and self-acceptance. It will give you a push to get on with things and encouragement to move on with things. It is great if you are looking for a change in direction.
CARROT (*Caucus carota*)	Carrot oil is wonderful to encourage a fresh new Daphne phase as it relieves stress and cleanses the mind. It is also a great oil for renewal and detoxing.
BERGAMOT (*Citrus bergamia*)	Bergamot oil is great for relieving depression and anxiety. It gives you a boost of confidence, helping you to overcome shyness and negative thoughts. It is also refreshing, uplifting, joyful and bright.
PINE (*Pinus sylvestris*)	Pine is a wonderful oil to help with confidence. It will invigorate a tired mind with its uplifting and refreshing scent and rejuvenate your concentration.
MANDARIN (*Citrus reticulata, C. nobilis*)	This beautiful citrus oil is uplifting and refreshing and will help you to overcome nervousness and tension. It's a light, happy, positive oil that will make you smile.
NUTMEG (*Myristica fragrans*)	Nutmeg oil will help you to get things started as it is great for warming and stimulating you into decisions. It is a warming and energising oil that will encourage you to get on with tasks.
LEMON (*Citrus medica limonum*)	Fresh and purifying, lemon oil can overcome any sluggish feelings. It is a purifying and fresh essential oil.
ROSEMARY (*Rosmarinus officinalis*)	Strengthening and restorative, rosemary oil helps to improve confidence, creativity and concentration and will make you feel as though you have found the elixir of youth. Use this oil when you have a lot to do and need to get things done.

ATLAS CEDAR (*Cedrus atlantica*)	This strengthening and powerful oil supports you in moving through situations such as focusing too much on the past and helps with anxiety and obsessive thoughts. It makes you feel strong in yourself and confident with decisions.
BASIL (*Ocimum basilicum*)	Use basil oil to overcome mental fatigue, negativity or lack of direction. Feel confident in your decisions and give yourself some clarity.
PETITGRAIN (*Citrus* X *aurantium* SUBSP. *amara*)	This beautiful citrus essential oil will assist you to restore energy and clarity. It is a balancing oil that helps you to overcome nervous exhaustion and mental fatigue. Feel uplifted, joyful, relaxed and move with self-confidence and optimism.

PHASE 2: DEMETER, DAYS 14 TO 17: BE EMBRACED

Demeter, who represents Mother Earth, is the goddess of agriculture, fertility, grain and the harvest. She has an association with human fertility, and there are many myths dealing with Demeter in her capacity as a fertility goddess. After Hades abducted her daughter, Persephone, Demeter began searching in vain, and her sorrow was so great that she denied herself all food, drink and comfort for nine days. She cursed the earth and harvest and the following year no seeds sprouted and no barley grew in the fields, and mortals were doomed to famine and eventual destruction if Demeter did not lift her curse.

A compromise was reached with Hades, and Persephone was allowed to return to Demeter for two-thirds of the year, with the remaining third of the year to be spent with her husband. Demeter was joyous and the earth began to swiftly recover its vitality and became fertile again. When Persephone is with Hades, the earth is wracked by the sorrow of her mother (winter). But when Persephone returns from the underworld to walk the earth again, Demeter pours forth the blessings of spring to welcome her beloved daughter home.

Demeter is in the days surrounding ovulation, which is generally a shorter phase than the others. Like Demeter this phase is one of motherly love, selflessness and practicality as she is nurturing, loving and accepting of everything around her. It is a more caring time when friends gravitate to you for support. Research supports the fact that in this phase self-esteem is significantly higher than it is in other phases of the menstrual cycle,[42] which is no surprise as it is a phase when energy levels and confidence are high and your skin feels fantastic.

Demeter is extremely non-judgemental and protective about the giving and receiving of love. She has a strong sense of self-worth and is content, competent and softly feminine and radiates love. The Demeter phase is the perfect time to host a dinner party at home. Your inner Demeter happily wants

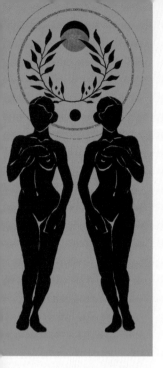

Give and receive love

to spend more time around the house, entertaining friends or beautifying your home and garden. You also may feel drawn to sitting under a tree in a park appreciating nature.

RELATIONSHIPS AND SEX

It is a time to both give and receive love, as Demeter's sensuality blossoms into an experience of deep love and sharing. A people magnet, you may find friends gravitating to you for your warmth, understanding and even some good advice during this phase.

Men may be attracted to your womanly, motherly essence. There is mounting evidence that ovulation prompts a range of subtle behaviours aimed at attracting the best possible mate. One study showed that women can unconsciously change their voices with the approach of ovulation, using a higher, more feminine pitch in social communication.[43] Another study outlined a shift in women's preferences for male traits such as more masculine faces and deeper male voices.[44]

There is a peak in sexual arousal in the days surrounding ovulation that then dips to quite low levels in the early Persephone phase and increases again just before menstruation.[45] Oestrogen levels reach a peak and the pituitary gland and hypothalamus release a surge of LH about midway through the cycle, which causes the mature follicle to rupture and the egg to be released into your fallopian tube; this is ovulation, which usually occurs around day 14 of the cycle. The egg begins to travel down the fallopian tube and into the uterus.

This is when a woman is most likely to become pregnant, and although this phase is often filled with joy and love, some women experience a dip in the middle of this phase. We are here to procreate. When females ovulate and progesterone levels climb as the body prepares for the egg to be fertilised: we're geared up to get pregnant. It may well be the last thing many of us want to do but it is how our bodies are wired. Once the opportunity to become pregnant has passed, you can experience a hormonally driven down day. Interestingly, a 2004 study featured in *Behavioural Ecology* found women in the ovulatory phase were more sexually attractive to males than were women in other phases.[46]

PHYSICAL WELL-BEING

Oestrogen levels skyrocket during ovulation, therefore you have an increase in energy, collagen production and metabolism. Some women have charted that one day around the middle of Demeter they experience tummy pain. This can be linked to ovulation, and you should chart it and seek some support if it continues to be a source of discomfort.

Demeter is sustaining, so it is common to feel as though your body can just power through the week. A lot of women experience Demeter as a positive phase that allows them to restore energy levels after the overly energetic Daphne phase. You will have stamina and endurance along with the capabilities to continue and nourish the exciting ideas created in the Daphne phase, recognising the responsibilities that are needed to complete any tasks.

SPORT, INJURIES AND PHYSICAL EXERCISE

You might want to train hard right after you stop bleeding because the spike in oestrogen that accompanies this phase will likely give you a boost of endurance. Research has found that women's knee joints tend to be looser during ovulation, which can make you vulnerable to an anterior cruciate ligament injury.

SKIN

Increased oestrogen can reduce sebum secretions and assist in collagen production, making your complexion appear more radiant, although some women experience minor breakouts due to the increased oestrogen levels. Keep this in mind and adjust your skin regime to suit if you need to. This is a phase of your cycle in which you will be likely to take a few risks, **but you should take one this month and give a new product a go.**

FOOD AND NUTRITION

The optimum food at this time of your cycle will assist the growth of a healthy follicle and egg and promote beneficial progesterone levels. Carbohydrate intake is still good and foods high in zinc and B vitamins are recommended.

BENEFICIAL FOOD	In general: carrot, dark leafy greens, beans, zucchini For zinc: seafood, spinach, pumpkin seeds, cashew nuts, cocoa and chicken For B vitamins: yoghurt, salmon, leafy greens, eggs For beta-carotene: carrots, sweet potatoes to promote cell growth and healthy ovulation
TO CURE THE CRAVING	Berries, coconut cream, garlic, raspberries, vanilla
AVOID	Dairy foods, completely raw foods, highly acidic foods
ESSENTIALS	B vitamins, calcium, magnesium, vitamin D, zinc

RISK APPETITE

You will be slightly less risk averse during ovulation than at other times of the month and thus more likely to take a risk and be less bothered about loss. Women most likely take risks during this high-fertility phase to increase the probability of attracting a partner.

EMOTIONS AND MOODS

As oestrogen increases so will your mood, energy and concentration as your body is preparing for ovulation. Your sex drive will also increase. You may feel more softly feminine and radiate love. Men may be attracted to you for your womanly, motherly essence, and at this time women dress to be more feminine and desirable to men. Women flock to Demeter for her warmth and understanding and even some good advice. She has strong self-worth and is happy, content and competent. In this phase self-esteem will be significantly higher than it is in other phases of the menstrual cycle.[47]

ALCOHOL

The reward centre of the brain is much more attuned to the pleasurable effects of alcohol when oestrogen levels are elevated around day 12 of your

cycle,[48] thus Demeter is the prime time for addictions to raise their ugly heads. Neurons in the brain in the ventral tegmental or 'reward' area are fired most rapidly in response to alcohol when women's oestrogen levels are high.[49] When oestrogen levels are high, alcohol is much more rewarding, and women may be more vulnerable to the effects of alcohol or more likely to overindulge or seek out alcohol during this phase.

SLEEP AND DREAMS

Sleep is usually uninterrupted in the first half of the cycle. Issues can begin after ovulation.

CONCENTRATION AND CREATIVITY

This can be a bit of a daydreamy time in which Demeter enjoys other people's company or sitting underneath a beautiful tree and staring up into the clouds. You should grab a blanket and do this yourself when you are in Demeter, as it feels great and will help to recharge your batteries. You may feel more in touch with nature and be drawn to gardening, entertaining at home, spending lots of time cooking

and beautifying your surroundings. This is the time to have a wonderful dinner party and invite your friends to show them how clever you are in the kitchen.

You may lose a little momentum in Demeter, but never fear: Persephone is around the corner and you will be back on track with gusto!

CLOTHING AND MAKE-UP

Demeter tends to wear womanly, flowing, feminine garments that accentuate her curves. She walks with a sway in her hips and scents her body with floral fragrances. In Demeter, women reported using a wider array of appearance-related products, which makes perfect sense given that these are the fertile phase days rather than luteal days.

Closer to ovulation women prefer clothing to be more revealing and sexy.[50] Near ovulation women also spend more time putting on their make-up and the estimated amount of make-up used is higher.

While remaining stylish, you may opt to wear more natural fibres, possibly ethnic styles and floral patterns or earthy colours, greens, rusts and browns. Your style may be less frilly and girly like Daphne and more feminine and flowing, and you won't be afraid to show a little cleavage if it feels right! You may feel drawn to cosmetics that have hues of pink or red. Your accessories would more likely be in the form of a carryall handbag with everything from headache tablets, pads (even though you don't need them at this time of the month), hairclips and writing paper.

CHAKRAS

The chakra most aligned to this phase is the heart chakra, or anahata. The heart chakra is aligned to love, forgiveness and compassion for yourself and others and is linked to the colours pink and green.

COLOURS

The colours that influence this phase are pinks and greens; a greater percentage of women selected pink or red when they were ovulating.[51] Pink represents unconditional love, warming and nurturing in its energy, while green represents healing and health. Linked with balance and harmony, wearing green or using it is some way will allow you to connect with those emotions and help you through this phase. As green is the colour of plants, it can play a part in reminding you to stop and breathe.

OILS

You will find floral and woody essential oils to be the most supportive in the phase, as they encourage compassion, confidence and connection with others.

ROSE (*Rosa x centifolia*)	Rose oil is all about being feminine: it is comforting and nurturing and helps to soothe sadness, rejection or loss. This oil is about beauty within and loving yourself.
CYPRESS (*Cupressus sempervirens*)	Cypress oil will provide support and protection from all that surrounds. It will help you to listen to others and not be dragged down with them.
EUCALYPTUS (*Eucalyptus citriodora*)	Eucalyptus oil is great for cooling heated emotions, clearing a muddled mind and washing away bad stuff. It will clear all negativity around you.

GERANIUM (*Pelargonium graveolens*)	Geranium oil is very harmonising and inspiring and will help to restore balance in your life. It has a really floral smell and allows you to connect with your feminine side.
LIME (*Citrus x aurantifolia*)	Lime oil is fresh, light, calming and relaxing and will help you deal with stress. It's a great conversation starter for when friends are around.
LAVENDER (*Lavandula angustifolia*)	Known as the 'mother oil', lavender helps with both the physical and emotional aspects of Demeter. This beautifully soothing, calming and nurturing oil supports you through stress, mental exhaustion, depression and burnout.
SWEET ORANGE (*Citrus x sinensis*)	Sweet orange oil will encourage an open heart and honesty and help you to embrace ideas and others with its warming, happy and yet energising effects. Use this oil to overcome burnout, obsessive thoughts, anxiety and worry.
CLARY SAGE (*Salvia sclarea*)	Clary sage's harmonising and restoring effects help to overcome depression, weepiness and guilt and encourage you to feel more grounded, confident, regenerated and strong yet calm.
VETIVER (*Vetiveria zizanioides*)	Vetiver oil is great for overcoming feelings of being overworked, anxiety, mental exhaustion and scattered thoughts. It helps to ground you, giving you feelings of support, strength and protection.
PATCHOULI (*Pogostemon cablin*)	Patchouli is a soothing and assuring oil that will help you to overcome depression, indecision and mood swings. It will also help you to feel restored, balanced and connected.
GERMAN CHAMOMILE (*Chamomilla recutita*)	Calm the mind and emotions by using German chamomile oil, which will help to soothe frayed nerves, irritability, temper and moodiness and any time you feel overly sensitive.

PHASE 3, PERSEPHONE, DAYS 18 TO 28: BE EMERGED

Persephone is the goddess of the underworld and the wife of Hades, who abducted Persephone while she was cavorting with her friends and picking flowers. During her time in the underworld Persephone fell in love with Hades and consummated the marriage, which is symbolised in mythology by the sharing of a fleshy pomegranate. Persephone remains somewhat elusive and can sometimes be seen to be overshadowed by her mother, Demeter. She is a good, loving daughter who has now tasted the fruits of sensuality and lust and is torn between loyalty to her mother, her husband and herself.

Hades engaged in an illicit affair with Minthe, and when Persephone found out about the relationship she kicked Minthe furiously. The gods transformed Minthe into a mint plant, and with each tread of Persephone's foot the plant released a minty scent.

This phase begins a day or two after ovulation and continues until three or four days before menstruation. Like Persephone, this phase is full of passion and emotion as she is incredibly intense and has somewhat irrational and passionate outbursts. Her sensuality and sexuality are expressed through creative outlets.

It is a time when she is not to be messed with and is often very effective in completing any necessary tasks at hand. Things that are requested from her will be completed merely to keep everything going her way. Persephone is also a time for a second wind created from passion. Whatever was discovered in Daphne and has been nurtured but not moved in Demeter will be kicked along once again by Persephone.

This phase is full of passion!

RELATIONSHIPS AND SEX

Persephone is a cracker of a phase: you will start to feel fuller in the boobs and look amazing, and you'll know it! Persephone has an animal magnetism that allows you to play with sexual prowess, taking joyous pleasures in the flesh and being decadent in her hedonism. You may find this time of sensuality is more direct and commanding or raw rather than flirtatious.

Sexual arousal during the luteal phase when progesterone is relatively high is significantly lower compared with the peaks around ovulation and the premenstrual and late menstruation days.[52] Five to six days before your period is the lowest for sexual arousal, with another peak in arousal two to three days before your period. With your hormones doing a dance within you, you can become unpredictable in the way you relate to others in relationships. As you will be more self-assured at this time you can be both very attractive and scary!

PHYSICAL WELL-BEING

This phase brings along some of the pre-menstrual aspects of our cycle, including some cramping, a swollen belly and tender breasts. You may feel lethargic due to the increased progesterone and body temperature. During the luteal phase a follicle containing an egg is released and the egg forms a corpus luteum, a mass of cells that forms in the ovaries and secretes high amounts of progesterone to prepare the lining of the uterus for implantation

or pregnancy. If the egg is not fertilised in the uterus then progesterone, oestrogen and testosterone levels will suddenly drop, causing the corpus luteum to degenerate and the lining of the uterus to be shed: this is menstruation.

As progesterone increases you are likely to experience a drop in mood and a lack of energy; you may feel lazy, lethargic and bloated. Some studies have likened progesterone effects to those of valium in the body. A surge of progesterone can also encourage depression and irritability while having physical impacts such as insomnia, water retention, slower digestion and even constipation.

Hormonal changes during this phase are often associated with fatigue and hunger, which might tempt you to skip your workouts. However, keeping active during the luteal phase can actually feel great if you're bloated and help to flood your body with happy hormones that can counterbalance the effects of your natural monthly process. Some Persephone phases bring a burst of energy, but towards the end of the phase you may feel exhausted which is why it is important to try and pace yourself during this time and keep your physical health in check.

You may feel more connected to your intuition and emotions, so be guided by them and don't be afraid to take a step back and focus inwardly when you need to. This can be a time when you become drained both emotionally and physically and your body needs rest. Taking extra time to sit in a nice spot and read is a great thing to do in Persephone.

SPORT, INJURIES AND PHYSICAL EXERCISE

Taking part in any form of exercise can be beneficial throughout Persephone as it can lower stress levels and lessen PMS symptoms. This could involve a boxing session or yoga, Pilates or a light aerobic session. If you choose a high-intensity workout make sure you allow time for rest afterwards as the inflammation in your body will be increased due to the drop of hormones, reducing your ability to recover quickly after a tough session. Progesterone increases core body temperature, so if you feel more puffed than usual don't stress – it could

just be hormones affecting your heart and breathing rates. Women have better coordination during the luteal phase, when their progesterone levels are high.

Normal adult women showed systematic performance fluctuations across the menstrual cycle on several motor and perceptual tests in performance. The mid-luteal phase, which is characterised by high levels of progesterone, was associated with improved performance on tests of speeded motor coordination and impaired performance on a perceptual-spatial test, compared with performance during menstruation. Variations in gonadal steroid levels may contribute substantially to the sex differences reported in human cognitive and motor skills.

As you move through this cycle and experience higher progesterone levels your muscle breakdown will increase. Protein should be prioritised in the 30-minute post-training window.

As research has suggested that arm curls are more effective during the luteal phase[53] you might want to focus on your upper body training and pepper it with some light lower body work. You should also train your upper body with pulls and presses throughout the month.

SKIN

Escalating progesterone encourages the production and secretion of higher amounts of sebum. The increase in body temperature plus excess oil can lead to breakouts and problem skin. My advice is to keep your skincare simple; I often use a few drops of tea tree or lavender essential oil. Keep your skin clean and use pure products that will help to settle the skin rather than aggravate it.

FOOD AND NUTRITION

In the luteal phase of the menstrual cycle women's energy intakes and expenditure are increased and they experience more frequent cravings for foods, particularly those that are high in carbohydrate and fat.[54] The decrease in hormones can trigger an inflammatory response, which is thought to be one cause of PMS symptoms. You may notice a change in your appetite as an increased desire for food such as sugar that can give you a lift.

To help reduce premenstrual symptoms, include B vitamins, essential fatty acids, healthy cholesterol and protein in your diet. If you are feeling more depressed or moody than usual increase your tryptophan, which is found in nuts, seeds, tofu, cheese, red meat, chicken, oats, beans and lentils. You may be lacking in vitamin B6, which helps to convert food to energy and assists in the production of serotonin and melatonin.

BENEFICIAL FOOD	Beetroot, carrot, cauliflower, dark leafy greens, mushrooms
TO CURE THE CRAVING	Berries, coconut cream, cacao, raspberries, vanilla
AVOID	Refined sugar, caffeine, carbonated drinks
ESSENTIALS	B vitamins, calcium, magnesium, tryptophan, zinc, healthy fat

RISK APPETITE

Toward the end of the luteal phase women are more loss adverse and less risky, preferring to play life by the rule book.

EMOTIONS AND MOODS

Persephone is aware of the dark and light aspects of her personality. It can be a time of destruction because she is so sensitive and feisty to all around her and is very quick to get frustrated and agitated. Self-esteem is lower and negative self-talk is higher during the premenstrual phase, compared with the ovulation phase where we are more self-confident.[55]

Persephone can be the time when emotions take over. It can bring out the best and worst in you, so it's important to be aware of this and take care of yourself. When you know how you are likely to be feeling, you can take steps to mitigate any negativity. Try to avoid taking on too much, and don't allow yourself to become overly sensitive. Give yourself permission to stop and take a breather before you react to people or situations and you'll find yourself responding to them in a better way.

A 2011 research paper questions the widespread idea that specific premenstrual dysphoria actually exists and states that things such as daily physical health status, perceived stress and social support explain daily mood better.[56] It showed the premenstrual phase by itself had no influence on mood in a random community sample of adult Canadian women studied over six months albeit with one marginally significant exception: mood was altered in the days of actually bleeding.

ALCOHOL

According to an international study that looked into the correlation between PMS and alcohol, having a few big nights out before your period could increase your symptoms of PMS by altering the levels of sex steroids and gonadotropin during the menstrual cycle.[57] PMS has previously been linked to fluctuations of these sex hormones during the cycle. The researchers found symptoms of PMS were more evident for heavy drinkers in particular.

What is heavy drinking? In the study a low intake of alcohol was defined as drinking less than one standard drink per day or consuming less than 10 grams of ethanol alcohol per day, while heavy drinking was putting away around one or more drinks containing about 10 grams of ethanol. I liked how this study acknowledged 'It was not clear whether this increase in the risk of PMS is due to the alcohol consumption or whether alcohol is consumed in an attempt to mitigate the symptoms of the syndrome' and suggests more study in needed in this area.

Another study conducted in 2011 showed distinct results: it confirmed the earlier findings that alcohol can enhance dysphoric mood effects including sadness, heaviness and numbness or sometimes irritability and mood swings in the luteal phase.[58]

SLEEP AND DREAMS

You may find that just prior to your period and during menstruation you suffer from sleep deprivation. In fact, 33 per cent of women say their slumber is negatively affected by their menstrual cycle. You can blame this lack of sleep on fluctuating hormones: when oestrogen and progesterone levels drop right before your period, it's common to have trouble sleeping due to hot flushes. Exhaustion from broken sleep plus a drop in serotonin can also occur at this time and can induce sugar cravings, so try to avoid sugar-rich and processed foods as these can stimulate sugar cravings.

In the luteal phase, due to increased progesterone levels, there is less REM sleep, which usually happens about 90 minutes after you fall asleep and is when your brain is most active. You may find that you dream more, whether it be while sleeping or that daydreaming comes much easier to you. Very vivid and colourful dreams can also occur at this time of the cycle.

CONCENTRATION AND CREATIVITY

Persephone is like having a second wind: there is potential for you to step up and complete tasks you perhaps began to implement in the previous two phases.

However, you need to manage yourself a little more in Persephone as you may get somewhat exhausted and have to plan short spurts of concentration rather than long marathon projects. Just make sure you take a break to rejuvenate before getting back into it again.

As your period gets closer, progesterone and oestrogen levels drop, causing mood changes and concentration problems. It is a wonderful time to bring out your creative side as Persephone calls on her inner thoughts to drum up ideas – music, painting, drawing, writing – anything she can sit alone and do. Persephone is passionate, so take advantage of such an inspirational time of the month, get your dancing shoes on and the paints out or cook up a divine meal you have wanted to create.

CLOTHING AND MAKE-UP

Persephone dresses in dark colours and soft, sensual fabrics, and wears low-cut fitted tops and long splits in her skirts or anything that will encourage womanly sensuality and desirability.

Wearing beautiful, slightly naughty underwear that no one else can see may be your go-to in this phase. Dark eye make-up, rich red lipstick and intoxicating perfume are all in order. You will look sensational in anything and feel great about it, not giving too much credence to what others think about you.

CHAKRAS

The chakras most aligned with this phase are the throat and third-eye chakras. The throat chakra, vishuddha, is related to will, self-expression, communication and expression. It is linked to the colour blue. The third-eye chakra, ajna, is related to mind, intuition, insight and wisdom and gives you more clarity in your thinking. It is linked to the colour indigo.

COLOURS

Blue is a great colour to represent your Persephone phase as it helps to promote intuitive thoughts and encourages sensitivity.

Blue is linked with the throat chakra so it is a great way to symbolise how you view frustration around communication issues.

Indigo can signify a protective nature, one you can wear if you need to shelter yourself and sit back more. Indigo is a very spiritual colour, and wearing it will signify a time of deep thought and inward expression.

OILS

This intense and passionate phase embraces some amazing scents. Soothing and calming oils are wonderful for keeping your negative temperament at bay.

GERMAN CHAMOMILE (*Chamomilla recutita*)	This lovely blue oil will calm and relax you and allow you to breathe deeply. It will encourage you to have patience with others and cool angry tempers.
ROMAN CHAMOMILE (*Anthemis nobilis*)	Roman chamomile oil is great for a busy head that keeps your mind active when you are trying to sleep.
MARJORAM (*Origanum majorana*)	For the overworked and irrational, marjoram oil will calm anxiety and crankiness and will soothe and calm your mind and emotions.
ROSEMARY (*Rosmarinus officinalis*)	Restore your emotions, boost your self-confidence and re-energise yourself with rosemary oil, a great pick-me-up that clears your head of muddled thoughts.
YLANG YLANG (*Cananga odorata*)	Feel great about who you are, enjoy your life and give your confidence a boost with ylang ylang oil, which is commonly used in perfumes. Like who you are!

JASMINE (*Jasminum* SPP.)	Jasmine oil can really take your breath away as it has a very strong fragrance. It is an exotic and mysterious oil that encourages femininity and love, allowing you to feel like a woman.
BERGAMOT (*Citrus bergamia*)	This refreshing and uplifting essential oil helps to overcome anxiety, burnout, stress, tension and emotional imbalances. Boost your self-confidence, motivation and concentration with bergamot oil.
SWEET ORANGE (*Citrus x sinensis*)	Sweet orange oil encourages an open heart and honesty and helps you embrace ideas and others with its warming, happy and yet energising effects. Use this oil to overcome burnout, obsessive thoughts, anxiety and worry.
ATLAS CEDARWOOD (*Cedrus atlantica*)	This strengthening and powerful oil supports you to move beyond focusing too much on the past and helps you to overcome anxiety and obsessive thoughts. It makes you feel strong in yourself and confident with your decisions.
PATCHOULI (*Pogostemon cablin*)	This soothing and assuring oil will assist you in overcoming depression, indecision and mood swings and help you feel restored, balanced and reasonable.
CLOVE (*Eugenia caryophyllus*)	Clove oil encourages and promotes healthy boundaries, helping you feel empowered and encouraged to break patterns of victimisation by honouring your own needs and speaking for yourself. Clove oil can also help with anxiety problems, promoting self-love and acceptance and helping you to not care as much about what others may think.
BLACK PEPPER (*Piper nigrum*)	This warming essential oil helps with emotional blockages, indecision, fatigue, anger and frustration. It will make you feel more comforted, strong and directional and give you more endurance and allow you to be more changeable and open.

| ROSE (*Rosa x centifolia*) | Considered to be one of the most beautiful essential oils in the world, rose oil helps you to feel passionate yet comforting and reassured. Use this essential oil for more confidence, sensuality and passion. |

PHASE 4, HECATE, DAYS 1 TO 5: BE EMBODIED

Hecate is the goddess of far-off places, roads and byways and had control over birth, life and death. She was the guardian of households and the protectress of all that was newborn. Although her powers also extended elsewhere she dwelt in the underworld, which was not the evil place it is considered to be today but was rather the resting place of the dead.

Often portrayed as a wise, old, all-seeing and all-knowing woman, Hecate could look in all directions: past, present and even the future. She was the only one of the Titans whom Zeus allowed to retain authority once the Olympians had defeated them, although Zeus only allowed Hecate the power of giving mortals anything she wished along with the power to withhold it. Because of her power she was represented as a triple form. Her main area of work was with the dead, night and darkness, witchcraft and the black arts.

This phase, commencing two to three days before menstruation and continuing for its duration, is epitomised by Hecate. Like Hecate, this phase is one of darkness, intuition and internal reflection. She interacts with her dreams, and feels she is part of the cycle of nature and intuitively recognises the patterns underlying it. She likes to withdraw and her energy levels are low, so she needs to slow down and rest more at this time of the month than any of the others.

RELATIONSHIPS AND SEX

As this is a more anti-social time, saying no to too many activities or social events will give you a good start. The energies of Hecate become more contained and focused inward, no longer seeking outward expression. You may prefer to spend your time in this phase reflecting on where you are and looking at what has been going on in your life.

You may not feel like any intimacy, but know that this doesn't have to be completely off limits if you are currently seeking connection with a partner.

PHYSICAL WELL-BEING

As you will be inward focused you may experience a need to not only express deep feelings of love and romance but to have these reciprocated by your partner, so reconnecting with them would be a wonderful thing to do in this cycle.

The first day of a woman's cycle period is considered to be the first day of the menstrual cycle, and if an egg has not been fertilised, it disintegrates. The levels of oestrogen and progesterone drop during this phase and cause the endometrium to break down and be shed in the form of menstrual blood. Bleeding lasts an average of five days. The worst of PMS is over, and some symptoms and especially breakouts subside.

Some women suffer from headaches, cramping and lower back pain while others feel quite rejuvenated, peaceful and calm. Menstrual migraine is a predominantly female disorder that women suffer from a day prior to and after their menstruation. According to *Therapeutic Advances in Neurological Disorders,* menstrual migraine is associated with menstrual stress.[59] However, menstrual migraines are classified in two categories: post-menstrual migraines, characterised by attacks in a menstruating woman, and menstrual-related migraines, which occur at other times of the month.

SPORT, INJURIES AND PHYSICAL TRAINING

Sport can feel harder at this time of the month: running five kilometres in 25 minutes may seem easy at some times of the month but can feel like a huge stretch

Reconnection with your partner would be a wonderful thing

when in Hecate. However, the anti-inflammatory and antioxidant properties of moderate exercise may help to reduce symptoms surrounding menstruation, leaving you feeling happier and more energised.

Generally speaking, it seems that emphasising lower body resistance training while you're menstruating and during the week and a half after you stop bleeding can help pack on strength gains and muscle. You can and should train your legs throughout the month, body permitting, as the kind of compound, full-body work leg training offers can help offset your cramps and provide a decent workout. Another compelling reason to train heavily during the week and a half after your period is that your body will have higher levels of oestrogen, which can lead to increased muscular endurance and

allow you to hit your muscle groups harder and more often.[60] At this time you'll want to emphasise any sprint work and high-intensity interval training you might like to do, as well because, again, those boosts in endurance can go a long way toward maximising your gains.

If you're someone who experiences dysphoria around menstruating, then training heavily during and especially right after might help combat its effects by increasing your sense of control over your body and musculature.

SKIN

During this phase you'll experience a decrease in temperature and sebum secretions. Your circulation will slow down and leave your skin a little dull and dry. **Avoid trying new products and focus on the basics of skincare,** using a gentle, natural-based cleanser and moisturising your skin, allowing it time to heal and soothe.

Using a simple cold-pressed oil such as apricot kernel or jojoba oil would be great. Jojoba has a similar molecular composition to sebum and is well absorbed by the skin.

FOOD AND NUTRITION

Your body will crave sugar on days one, two and three as it experiences drops in progesterone, oestrogen and testosterone levels. The strong decrease in the levels of the mood-stabilising chemicals serotonin and dopamine leading up to and during your period will prompt you to reach for the chocolate, lollies and cakes as well as refined carbs. To combat this you may need mood-stabilising foods, so a diet with increased tryptophan, B-complex vitamins, essential fatty acids and iron-rich leafy green vegetables will be beneficial.

Tryptophan-containing foods include a host of seeds such as pumpkin, squash, chia, sesame and sunflower, as we all roasted soybeans, tofu, reduced fat mozzarella cheese, parmesan and cheddar cheeses, lamb, beef, pork, chicken, turkey, cooked tuna, cooked crab, uncooked oat bran and oats, beans and lentils and whole eggs.

Increasing anti-inflammatory foods can also be of great benefit. Include foods rich in vitamin D, calcium, fish and B vitamins. Look to improve circulation with vitamin E from avocado, pumpkin seeds, trout and red peppers. Lower the consumption of animal products, dairy foods and high-fat meat to reduce bloating and inflammation. Your body's drop in temperature means warm soups and hearty food should also be on the menu.

BENEFICIAL FOOD	Fish, apples, avocado, banana, broccoli, carrot, cucumber
TO CURE THE CRAVING	Cacao, dates, pumpkin seeds, ginger
AVOID	Refined sugar, dairy foods, high-sodium foods
ESSENTIALS	Iron, B vitamins, vitamins C, D and E, calcium

RISK APPETITE

You will be feeling more vulnerable and internally reflective in this phase, so it's no surprise that risk appetite is low. This is a time to be slow and steady and more thoughtful in your decision-making.

EMOTIONS AND MOODS

During this phase you will be fully aware of your body and conscious of bleeding. Although you may be withdrawn, this phase is not a negative one but carries a sense of acceptance and inner strength. There is evidence that suggests an exacerbation of paranoia around menstruation in women who suffer from PMS.[61]

On the positive side of Hecate is the ability to really assess what is going on with your life. Even if you are shrouded in a black mood, it is a time when you can listen to your internal voices and let go of all things that are draining your precious energy.

Don't make any rash decisions in Hecate. Take the time to sit down and look at what is happening in your work, relationships and health, then think about what is worth keeping and what you want to let go of. This is a wonderful time to release anything from your life that is no longer serving you and reconnecting with yourself, taking long, indulgent baths with a wonderful blend of essential oils or going for a relaxing facial or massage.

ALCOHOL

Tolerance for alcohol will be a little lower during this phase. Often alcohol can exacerbate any health issues around menstruation such as cramping, bloating or even feeling sick, and especially affect sleep. If you are struggling with settling or feeling low and flat I suggest you take a break from the booze.

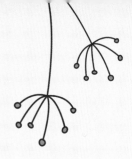

SLEEP AND DREAMS

I'm sure many of you will not be surprised to hear me say that sleep is fairly poor in the first couple of days around menstruation. This is usually linked to common menstrual problems: mainly cramps, bloating, headaches, heavy bleeding and pain. Women report worse sleep during the days prior to and during the first few days of their period.

During this phase testosterone, oestrogen and progesterone are at their lowest, meaning you feel like resting or having quiet time. Getting extra rest will allow you to interact with dreams and daydream more, so allow your mind to run wild with wonderful thoughts and images.

As mentioned in Persephone, your dreams can get a little wild right before your period, so make note of what you experience and see if you can find a deeper meaning or connection to what your subconscious mind is trying to tell you. Your dreams could be a hodgepodge of Dr Seuss–worthy comedy, but there may also be some incredible insights if you take the time to reflect.

Sleep can be incredibly healing, so make sure you schedule in good rest and do what you can to ensure the best night's sleep.

CONCENTRATION AND CREATIVITY

In this phase, everyday tasks can seem mundane and you may find it harder to concentrate and be slower thinking and a little illogical or even chaotic in your

thoughts. Despite this, Hecate is a great time for reflection so it would be nice time to sit back and reflect on your world. Your creative energy may be more internal rather than external.

Although this is a phase in which you will sometimes struggle with verbal communication (as opposed to Demeter, where it is your strength), studies have shown there are increased abilities around special awareness tasks. In short, this means you will be better at doing tasks such as map reading or learning a complex skill for which you need good hand-eye co-ordination.

CLOTHING AND MAKE-UP

Comfort is the main focus for Hecate: clothes may be old faithfuls that are easy to wear or free flowing or loose-waisted clothes such as skirts or dresses. Your undies may look more like Bridget Jones' knickers and less like tooth floss. In fact, these outfits may never see the light of day at any other time of the month!

Hecate doesn't tend to feel really great in those outfits she had on just a few days ago, and won't even try to push herself to wear the bold, bright lipstick she has in her handbag from last week's night out.

CHAKRAS

The chakras most aligned to this phase are the base and crown chakras. The base chakra, muladhara, is related to the material world and strengthens the reproductive system. It is related to the colour red. The crown chakra, sahasrara, is related to the colour violet and to spirituality, and represents enlightenment and self-realisation.

COLOURS

You may find yourself leaning towards colours like reds, blacks and purples. Red symbolises the colour of life and of blood, black indicates a time of withdrawal and purple expresses a more mysterious nature.

The energy red gives is one to help when you are feeling run down or withdrawn. Wearing red will keep you connected to the earth. Violet is excellent to wear if you are seeking spiritual development at this time of your cycle as it gives you strength at a time of feeling low and can allow you to connect with yourself on a deeper level so you feel balanced and calm.

OILS

Look for essential oils that will support rest and relaxation through deepening your breathing, calming your nervous system and building your confidence.

JUNIPER BERRY (*Juniperus communis*)	Juniper is the oil to use when you feel as though you are being attacked from all angles, as it offers emotional protection and helps to cleanse you from all that's around you. Be strong!
LAVENDER (*Lavandula angustifolia*)	Lavender is a great oil for Hecate as it is soothing, calming and nurturing. It can help calm you and make you feel comfortable in your own space.
FRANKINCENSE (*Boswellia carterii*)	Frankincense oil is for restoration and being still. It has a wonderful reputation of encouraging meditation, giving internal wisdom and helping the development of intuition.
AUSTRALIAN SANDALWOOD (*Santalum spicatum*)	Sandalwood oil develops inner strength and trust in your intuition. Use it to counteract anxiety, nervous tension and selfishness and supports you to feel warm, comforted and serene yet sensual.
GRAPEFRUIT (*Citrus grandis*)	This time of the month can invoke emotions such as anger and resentment, and grapefruit oil can clear these and make you feel happy and refreshed. It is a good oil for a bad day.

YLANG YLANG (*Cananga adorata*)	You deserve to feel good about yourself, so boost your confidence, enjoy yourself and love who you are with ylang ylang oil.
CLARY SAGE (*Salvia sclarea*)	Sage oil's harmonising and restoring effects help to overcome depression, weepiness and guilt and encourages you to feel more grounded, confident, regenerated and strong and yet calm.
FRANGONIA (*Agonis fragrans*)	This unique Australian essential oil helps create a beautiful balance and is often used for calming and intuitive healing.
LEMON (*Citrus medica limonum*)	This fresh and purifying oil can overcome sluggish feelings, so if you are lacking motivation it will help you get things done.
PATCHOULI (*Pogostemon cablin*)	This soothing and assuring oil helps you to overcome depression, indecision and mood swings. Patchouli oil will assist you to feel restored, balanced, reasonable and connected.
GERANIUM (*Pelargonium graveolens*)	Geranium oil is very harmonising, inspiring and balancing, and its floral smell allows you to connect with your feminine side.
CYPRESS (*Cupressus sempervirens*)	Cypress oil provides protection and support and helps you to listen to others and not be dragged down by them.
ATLAS CEDARWOOD (*Cedrus atlantica*)	This strengthening and powerful oil supports you to move beyond focusing too much on the past, anxiety and obsessive thoughts. It will make you feel strong in yourself and confident with your decisions.

THE FOUR GODDESSES IN SUMMARY

	DAPHNE	DEMETER	PERSEPHONE	HECATE
WHEN IN THE CYCLE?	Days 6 to 13	Days 14 to 17	Days 18 to 28	Days 1 to 5
EMOTIONS/ MOODS	Harmonious, happy, positive	Peaceful, harmonious, loving, motherly	Intense, sensual, passionate, irritable	Peaceful, irritable, psychic, teary
ENERGY LEVELS	Happy, social, dynamic, energetic	Social, calm, dynamic	Strong, powerful, frustrated, emotional	Flat, cranky, unsociable, reflective
PHYSICAL HEALTH	Light, cleansed	Light cramps	Swollen or tender breasts, bloated	Fatigue, swollen belly, cramps
CLOTHING	White, pastels, lacy, sporty, fitted	Florals, feminine, sexy, lacy	Sensual fabrics, low cut, firm/ sexy, bright red	Comfortable, old favourites, stretchy fabric
BENEFICIAL FOOD	Asparagus, pumpkin, sweet potato, peas, figs, lemon	Carrot, dark leafy greens, beans, zucchini	Beetroot, carrot, cauliflower, dark leafy greens, mushrooms	Apples, avocado, banana, broccoli, carrot, cucumber

	DAPHNE	DEMETER	PERSEPHONE	HECATE
CURE THE CRAVING	Vegetable chips, dates, popcorn, peanut butter	Berries, coconut cream, garlic, raspberries, vanilla	Berries, coconut cream, cacao, raspberries, vanilla	Cacao, dates, pumpkin seeds, ginger
AVOID	Refined sugar, alcohol	High-fat dairy food, completely raw foods, highly acidic foods	Refined sugar, caffeine, carbonated drinks	Refined sugar, dairy, high sodium foods
ESSENTIALS	B vitamins, iron, magnesium, Omega 3 fatty acids	B vitamins, calcium, magnesium, vitamin D, zinc	B vitamins, calcium, magnesium, tryptophan, zinc, healthy fat	Iron, B vitamins, vitamins C, D and E
COLOURS	Orange, yellow	Pink, green	Red, blue, indigo	Red, violet
CONCENTRATION	Focused, clear, sharp	Steady, calm	Scattered, intense	
CREATIVITY		Steady	Heightened, renewed, creative	

	DAPHNE	DEMETER	PERSEPHONE	HECATE
SCENTS	Lemon, bergamot, rosemary, nutmeg	Lavender, clary sage, geranium, vetiver	Bergamot, sweet orange, Roman chamomile, ylang ylang	Clary sage, frankincense, juniper, lavender
RISK AND LOSS		High		Low
SLEEP			May be affected or broken	May be disrupted due to cramps and other menstrual symptoms

Now you have uncovered the four phases and seen how truly powerful they are. Did you notice any resemblance in the descriptions of the goddesses and how you feel at certain times in your cycle? It is common for the traits of the goddesses and their respective impacts to overlap slightly between the phases, but the more you chart your cycle the clearer your individual picture will become.

Are you ready to learn how to harness the power of charting to assist you in embracing your emgoddess? Read on, lovely lady.

· ❋ CHAPTER 3 ❋ ·

Embody: CHARTING YOUR MOODS AND EMOTIONS

∽∾∾∾∾ ⊱⊰ ⊱⊰⊱⊰⊰⊰

A t its core Emgoddess is a form of mindfulness: you take the time to sit and think about how you feel physically and emotionally. Is your body sore and tender or powerful and flexible? Are you happy, full of energy, calm and centred, passionate and powerful or inward and reflective?

After you sit and listen to your body, you colour in your chart to secure the process. What colours are you drawn to today? How much do you want to write? Do you even want to chart today? Just being aware of these different feelings and emotions will contribute to the process of mindfulness.

An entire stress-reduction program with decades of experience and tens of thousands of practitioners is an excellent indication that mindfulness works. Mindfulness is considered to be a key element in fighting stress and regulating emotions and there are numerous studies that back up this idea, with one on present-moment awareness finding it facilitates an adaptive response to daily stressors.[62] Another study found that mindfulness, more so than relaxation or self-affirmation controls, produces less avoidance and more approach coping as a response to stress.[63]

In a world of daily stress, anxieties and expectation, the mind can come under a lot of pressure, which directly affects mood and makes you less positive and somewhat disconnected from yourself. Meditation has a profound, rich and calming effect on the body, clears your mind and advocates feelings of peace and a sense of awareness. It is a chance to tap into an abundance of creative energy to give a more meaningful experience of life that will enrich you permanently.

For me, charting is definitely a form of mindfulness. I take my pencils and pens and my charting calendar and find a quiet place to sit for moment. I close my eyes, take a deep breath and ask myself: *How do I feel emotionally and physically?* I wait a moment, then open my eyes and start to write, draw and colour. I use essential oils sometimes to enhance the process by popping a few drops of one of the Emgoddess essential oils into a diffuser.

Therapists from many disciplines recommend journalling your emotions as a means of processing your thoughts, dealing with situations or simply connecting to your inner self. The Emgoddess approach of charting takes this concept much further to gain a true sense of all you are, highlighting the connection between your menstrual cycle and your emotions.

Recording your cycle is beneficial in many ways: it will help you to understand how your cycle impacts every aspect of your life, no matter where you are in the cycle. A healthy cycle equals a healthy you. Its regularity will show you that your body is working well, then whenever there are unusual disruptions, you will uncover them first through your charts, which will give you an incredible heads-up on potential health

challenges long before they become a major problem. You should chart because:

Charting is fun!

- It's fun!
- It reduces stress: it has been proven that charting or keeping a journal helps to reduce the impact of stress.
- It minimises feelings of distress: understanding your perceptions at each phase of the month can reduce feelings of distress and paranoia,[64] which ultimately allows you to guard against times of increased negative thoughts.
- It allows you to let go, giving you more clarity.
- It allows you to increase focus and energy: taking the time to chart your feelings and emotions can help you see exactly what is happening in your life and how it is affecting you. It can help you separate the big stuff from the little things that may be bothering you.
- It's a therapeutic way of reconnecting you to your thoughts and emotions as well as physical symptoms.
- It's a simple and creative outlet that anyone can do: it's as simple as colouring in!
- It identifies key times of your month: through charting you'll see patterns emerge.

It is hard to appreciate and work with your menstrual cycle if you do not stop to listen every now and then. Organise your month around your menstrual patterns.

FEEDBACK FROM A ROCKIN' RETIREE

I have always been pretty comfortable with my body. You could call me a bit of a hippy in my day. I still continue to do a lot of meditation and yoga and try to keep my body and mind healthy. I attended a special event at my yoga class. Sharon came along to share with us about out menstrual cycles and how they impact us.

I haven't had a period for a few years now. I am through the other side of menopause, but I wanted to attend as I was interested to hear what this was all about.

I was shocked.

Everything Sharon said made complete sense; it was like all this information was clicking into place. 'Why am I hearing this for the first time,' I asked. This information would have been so beneficial as a younger woman, rather than going through life navigating the changes and challenging my thoughts constantly along the way.

I know I still have a cycle of sort. Sure, it's different; I don't have a period and my ups and downs are less extreme. But I know I still have a cycle. So Sharon suggested I chart using the phases of the moon.

I just love it. I chart a new chart each new moon, and I chart all the things that are important to me: my creativity, my focus and my energy levels. After a year of charting I can see the patterns in my life.

I am confident in my own skin and this charting helps me stop and mindfully appreciate what my body continues to give me each month. This process has made me very grateful to be the woman that I am.

What is involved in charting? Each month you will experience highs and lows, joy and sadness and vitality and lethargy, and charting involves recording all of these moods, emotions, energy levels, dreams, clothing and make-up choices, sensitivities, food preferences, friends you gravitate to and general health and attitudes on a day-to-day basis in a pie chart using words, pictures and colours. Through this process you will learn to read your body in a new and respectful way: when you are best able to take on new projects and when your body needs rest.

Taking the time to acknowledge, accept and even celebrate the changes you experience throughout each cycle can have unexpected benefits in many areas of your life. Public campaigns and education about menstruation have been successful in reducing other female health conditions, while one article[65] showed how education campaigns helped to reduce the rates of hysterectomies by 25.8 per cent to 33.2 per cent. These numbers indicate psychological factors play a major role in the perception of menstruation and menstrual symptoms, and that when educated about the issues, women feel free to openly talk about them with practitioners, friends and family and make better judgements. Sharing information and asking questions will help you to normalise an openness about and acceptance of the menstrual cycle. You can then derive a sense of belonging and of meaning and purpose to your cycle, which will have a strong impact on self-perception and emotional well-being.[66]

I suggest you purchase a folder and collate all your charts inside. Over time you will develop a clear picture of your cycle and the patterns that regularly appear. By looking through the months, you will identify the times you show the same emotions, feelings and energy levels and be able to plan accordingly for the month ahead. It would be a good idea as Emgoddess becomes a way of life to also record your temperature on a chart; you can take this information to your health practitioner if needed, so they can also see what is happening in your body. For example, you may plan to skip the gym during low-energy times and book a massage instead, or you may ensure that tricky family dinners fall in your more nurturing and entertaining phase. It is a therapeutic way of reconnecting your physical, emotional and spiritual self, and a simple, creative and fun outlet anyone can do.

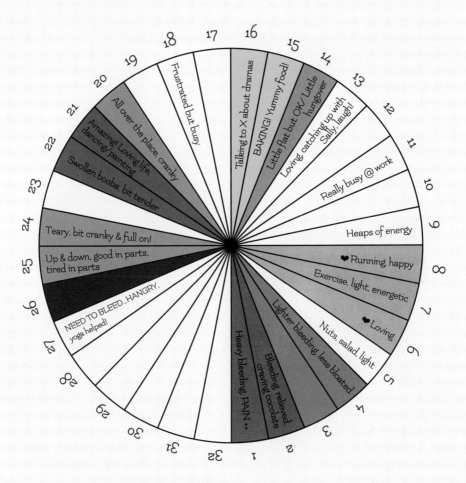

Step 1, download the chart: I recommend using a pie chart similar to the Emgoddess pie chart illustrated here; you can download a free chart from the Emgoddess website. You can also purchase a charting calendar from the website. If you do download the chart, make sure you pop your charts into a folder and leave them with some pencils somewhere handy such as beside your bed.

Step 2, prepare your chart: you will need a new chart for the first day of your cycle; thus the first day of your period will be the first day of your new chart. I highly recommend on this first day of your cycle you write up your entire chart. Each section of the pie chart represents a day in your cycle; the circle is divided into 32 sections to allow for different cycle lengths you may experience from month to month. If your cycle is longer than 32 days simply divide a few of the sections to make extra days. If you're like me and you have a shorter cycle, simply black out the chocks you don't need.

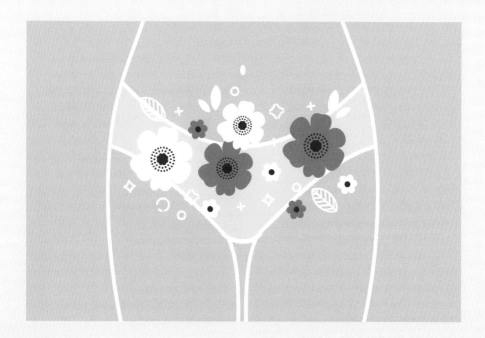

Start the diagram by shading in day 1 (at the bottom of the chart). This day represents the first day of your cycle and therefore the first day of menstruation. Moving anti-clockwise, label each segment with the day of the cycle and of the month. I write up the full month, so when I come to chart, I just have to think about how I feel and write it in. I recommend you do this because it makes the process quick and simple and because sometimes you will have a couple of days when you do not chart because you get busy, go away and forget to take your chart with you or you might just not feel like it, and that's okay. When you return to your chart, if all the dates and days are in, you can easily find where you are and start again. You may wish to reflect on some of the days you missed and put in a few words on how you felt.

Enter the moon cycle with a coloured-in circle for a new moon and an empty circle for a full moon.

Step 3, beginning to chart: this is your time, so express yourself and feel free to chart however is right for you. If you need a little inspiration, have a look at the example chart on page 121. Chart for a minimum of six to 12 months, which will allow you to see the patterns showing up in your cycle. It is a five-minute job each day and is time that can be used for precious moments of reflection where you can breathe calmly and truly get in touch with how you have felt and what you have experienced each day. Within each month your emotions will fluctuate: sometimes you will be a homebody while at other times you will be an independent, world-savvy woman. Keep track of these fluctuations, filling them in on your chart so you can understand them and express yourself and ultimately have the best fun you can within your cycle.

When filling in your chart try to use the same words and colours each month, which will make it easy for you to compare months. Compose a key to remind yourself of the words or colours you like to use, and remember this is your chart so you can mould it and change it as you change. Once you've done this, you can start on the fun stuff!

WHO CAN CHART?

Lots of women don't have periods yet they still have cycles. The Emgoddess program will work for them, too, and here's how:

While on the contraceptive pill: although contraceptive pills completely influence your natural hormonal cycle, you still move through the four phases. Chart your cycle based on the dates of your pill: day 1 in your cycle will be day 1 in your Emgoddess app or chart.

Some people may think that because you are using the contraceptive pill and are not meant to ovulate you will not have the ups and downs of emotions. However, I have yet to meet a woman who doesn't have the odd down day. Although a woman's emotions can be linked to the increase and decrease of hormones through the body throughout the month, there can be other factors that impact emotions, and you may be surprised to find how often they form a cycle. It is just as important for you as a woman on the pill to listen to your body and chart your daily expressions.

While using other contraceptive devices or you don't have a cycle: about 16 per cent of women in Europe, Australia and the USA use a form of contraception that stops their period entirely,[67] or you may be peri-menopausal or post-menopausal. If you are one of these women you can still chart using the cycle of the moon, which roughly equates to the days in a woman's cycle.

Day 1 in this cycle is the first day of the new moon, the time you would normally begin menstruating, so chart day 1 of a new moon as day 1 in your cycle. The full moon marks the middle of the cycle, when you would be ovulating. It's easy to remember: new moon = new chart.

While pregnant: there are three stages of life women journey through. Beginning as a young maiden, this phase is commonly known as our youth. The next phase is the phase of the enchantress, a feisty and passionate woman driving on her chosen path. The third phase is known as the crone or wise woman phase, which leads into menopause. In between these phases some women experience a fourth phase known as the mother phase, where they are pregnant.

Pregnancy is a whole journey in itself, one of new discoveries and inner connection. This phase is not influenced by the same monthly cycle as that of a woman who is menstruating and therefore doesn't commonly have regularity to it. Should you feel like you are all over the place and would like to see if there is

a pattern, continue to use the Emgoddess app or charts for self-reflection, although you may also like to take this time off from charting and enjoy what pregnancy brings you at this special time of life.

IS CHARTING BETTER THAN USING AN APP?

I know apps make life a bit quicker and simpler when charting your cycle, being a quick way to see what day you are on and when you are due for your next period. However, handwriting your chart has more power and this is why: many of us are looking for a deeper connection to different parts of our world, such as with the local community, or in relationships, and many of us are looking for a better connection to self. When I speak to women at various forums I hear many reflecting on who they are as people and wanting to discover more about how they tick. I believe you will derive greater satisfaction using colours and patterns on a chart and journalling your thoughts as part of your charting ritual than you will from using an app.

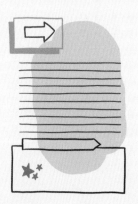

WHAT TO CHART

You can record whatever you feel is relevant to your world, although listed on the following pages are some of the common elements I recommend capturing along with an explanation and key words to give you ideas.

General physical health: listing all the physical changes you face every month is a simple way for beginners to chart. Record skin breakouts, tender or swollen breasts and other physical symptoms you recognise as they occur. Are you clumsy or forgetful at one time or another? Be sure to also chart headaches and migraines, which can be linked to your menstrual cycles.

Key words: fatigue, quality of sleep, food cravings, physical changes such as breast swelling, bloating, physical pain.

Energy levels: record the differences in energy levels you have within each month as it is great to see when you have more energy and are more outgoing and compare those to other times of the month when you are feeling quite low in energy. Look at when you have felt like being alone, being intimate with someone, or going out to a party with as many people as you can possibly get around you.

Key words: dynamic, sociable, low, flat, withdrawn, unsociable, enthusiastic, energetic.

Emotions and moods: although we all have fluctuating emotions and moods, some women may not change as dramatically as others, so it is important to be aware of your subtle changes. There is no doubt, however, that moods are never consistent throughout the month; you are only human, after all! Notice how you act towards others and yourself. Are there times of the month when you

have an abundance of patience, gladly spending time helping someone get something right, and other times when you are readily irritated and impatient? Look at not only who you are keen to spend time with but also who is searching you out. Do loads of friends need advice around the same time or someone to go and party with?

Key words: peaceful, harmonious, angry, irritable, loving, motherly, psychic, cranky, teary, happy.

Nutrition: we all know we absolutely crave certain foods at different times of the month. It doesn't have to be junk food: you may really long for a good healthy salad or vegies. Food is such an important aspect of your overall health that noting the foods you are eating throughout the month can really help to identify if you are lacking or craving certain vitamins and minerals.

Key words: sugar, carbs, fruits, vegies, salad, ice-cream, super hungry, nibbling, no appetite.

Sleep and dreams: sleep is important, as you well know, and it's quite possible you will experience disturbed sleep around menstruation. You may feel extremely tired or be up and down all through the night. Make sure you keep track of your sleep patterns and chart any changes that seem out of the ordinary for you.

Dreams play a significant part in your subconscious. Is there a time in your cycle where your dreams are more vivid or wild? Charting doesn't require you to analyse your dreams, but it can be useful to note whether you remember them more at certain times and whether there is a repetitive message or theme.

Key words: sensuality, interaction with others, strong colours, animals, magical content, predictive or psychic dreams, recurring dreams.

Outward expression: what activities are you drawn to at different times of your cycle? Look at whether you are more interested in going out, playing sport or staying at home, baking or reading a good book. What is your confidence like? Look at how others around you affect your thoughts and feelings.

Subtle forces guide the expression of your sensual self, and let's not stop with clothing. Think about your choices of fragrance, jewellery, make-up and hair. One of my very good friends wears one particular lipstick only during a particular phase of her cycle just to get into the fun of it! Through image, colour and shape you reflect and express your goddess energies.

Key words: sporting pursuits, confidence, how you dress.

Concentration and creativity: are you really organised and focused at different phases of the month? Do you feel like this more than once in the month?

Key words: free, in flow, creative, expression, liberated, unchained, blocked, constricted, muse.

Scents: it is amazing how your sense of smell can change during your period, and you may find you smell something one week and love it but the next week you can't stand the smell. Your hormones can affect your sense of smell, and different hormones impact both how you smell and what you're smelling.

Pay attention to whether any smells really attracted you or made you recoil during the day; you may see some patterns emerge over time. Emgoddess has created a selection of specially formulated essential oil blends that are compatible with each of the four phases, which you can check out at www.emgoddess.com.au.

Pay attention to smells

Key words: floral, sweet, pungent, musky, woody, fruity.

Self-awareness: we can be our own worst enemies at certain times of the month. Observe those times when you are super harsh and those times when you're pretty stoked or proud of yourself. By charting this you will learn to nourish yourself a bit more when you are feeling low and look back at why you were so happy with who you were only a few days ago.

Key words: low, harsh, comfortable, confident, unsure.

Colour: colour has been used throughout history to link us with different images, for example, it is common to think of the bright, vibrant sun when you see yellow, the calm and tranquil ocean when you see blue and spirituality when you see purple. After you have filled your sections with words to describe your feelings, you may wish to use colours in your chart to signify emotional states, which will provide an easy visual gauge to identify emerging trends. Using colour to signify an emotional state for you will be an easy way of looking at previous charts to see how you were feeling.

These are the colours I use to represent my feelings:

- Red is an obvious colour to represent menstruation and is playful, stimulating, passionate, aggressive and important.
- Orange represents joy, creativity, warmth and vibrancy and is a good way to add excitement.
- Yellow is happy, friendly, fun, energetic and joyful and is able to stimulate and revitalise.
- Green is balanced, harmonising, natural and earthy and usually represents the natural environment and outdoors.
- Blue represents inner calm, creative expression, serenity, trustworthiness and invitation.
- Purple is mysterious, romantic, passionate, deep and cooling for when you feel frustrated.
- Pink represents self-love, femininity, girliness and softness and is traditionally used with love and romantic themes alongside red and light purple.

- Brown is earthy, sturdy and rustic and is associated with the earth and trees.
- Black is powerful, sophisticated, edgy, dark, repressed and closed and adds an air of mystery.
- White is clean, virtuous, healthy, powerful and focused and gives off a clean, chaste impression.
- Grey is neutral, formal and gloomy.

Whatever colours you choose, just pick ones that represent your emotions, moods and feelings.

FEEDBACK FROM A DAD

I knew my daughter was growing up and life as we knew it was going to change. I also knew one day she would get her period but, to be honest, I never really gave it much thought as I presumed it would be something she spoke to her mum about. What would I know?

But one day I was in a store in the city and was introduced to Sharon and Emgoddess. She explained to me the four phases of the menstrual cycle and how they will impact my daughter. We had a good laugh, but it actually really made sense. Obviously living with her mum made me think of all the situations that I could relate to with her cycle.

Sharon explained how this knowledge is so important and powerful, but one statistic really struck me between the eyes: one research paper showed young women who are comfortable with their bodies and menstrual cycles are more likely to be confident with their bodies as older women. These women were less likely to be in vulnerable or promiscuous situations and more confident in decisions around their bodies. Sign me up! I say.

I saw this as an opportunity to help share in a journey with my teenage daughter rather than leaving it to something solely between her and her mum. I read through all the material and I love it. I understand the phases and sometimes I can see what phase my daughter is in before she realises!

I use this information to be a good dad. I know when to push and when to lay off and, most importantly, when to pick up some extra chocolate on the way home from work.

You don't have to spend hours charting or even fill your chart in every day. Sometimes you won't feel like expressing yourself through writing, which could be saying something in itself. I keep a folder and a pencil case full of different colours by my bed and chart just before drifting off to sleep.

Within four to six months of charting patterns will emerge. This information is truly powerful as it allows you to plan and be in better control of how you deal with situations based on how you feel. What you may not yet have noticed, though, is that during the month you have four very strong influences. It's time to discover how these phases appear in your cycle and how to utilise their positive aspects to enhance your life.

CHAPTER 4

Empower: USING YOUR RESULTS TO LEAD YOURSELF AND OTHERS

~~~~~~~~~~~~~~~~~~~~

S
o what now, you may ask. You have all this newfound knowledge, and you have taken the time to discover what your cycle means to you and how it influences your mood and self-esteem. You have looked into your individual cycle and really discovered what happens to you at different times of the month and how you can look at the different phases in a positive rather than negative way.

Once you have charted for six months or more you will notice patterns appearing. You now understand how to chart and what to chart and the power of charting. You have read through each of the four phases in detail that show you the good, bad and ugly of each phase. Hopefully by now you are identifying some key attributes that show up for you during your four phases and seeing how you can tap into the strengths of the different phases to achieve incredible results for your health and well-being.

If you are in business you can become more mindful of when to plan high-powered meetings and when to shut the door and focus on smashing out those intricate projects. If you are an athlete, you can become more aware of where you are in your cycle each time you train or compete, allowing you to take the appropriate physical and mental steps to ensure you are performing at your best. If you are a stay-at-home mum, you can schedule play dates at times when you feel more energised and prepared for social interaction. When you are more introverted, you can spend a day with crafts scattered across the floor having one-on-one time with your little ones.

The applications for Emgoddess are limitless, and you now have the tools you need to begin empowering yourself to greatness. This is your first step in breaking the long-held tradition in many families of perpetuating the negative assumptions and misconceptions about menstruation, myths and taboos that likely caused the shame many women feel about this natural process. The external perceptions of menstruating women, such as their being less sexy, more irritable and more motherly than non-menstruating women, can only enhance these feelings of shame.

A 1985 survey conducted on teenage women in Australia found that 80 per cent considered menstruation to be inconvenient or embarrassing, and the majority lacked sufficient information about menstruation and ovulation.[68] It was more recently reported that little support is provided to girls living in poverty as they reach period age, the result being that many have negative experiences that can be associated with depression, delinquency and substance abuse.[69] Gaps in puberty education can have serious consequences for adolescent decision-making about sex and family planning. In lower-income countries, girls face considerable challenges in managing menstruation during school, with some even resorting to transactional sex to purchase sanitary products.

Since mothers are a key source of information for young girls when they go through puberty, it is likely that women who feel shame about their reproductive functions pass this attitude on to their daughters. Therefore, the education of men and women of all ages is an important goal to overcome the menstrual shame felt by women around the world. The Empowerment Cycle has an online program created by Emgoddess that encourages healthy, positive views of menstruation and breastfeeding by debunking myths and discussing women's concerns about their reproductive functions. In addition, this program can educate mothers and teachers to ensure that the right messages are getting through to children.

Now is the time for you to set off on the path of discovery towards menstrual health empowerment. Let's break these chains so we can emerge into a future in which our natural process is once again celebrated for the wonder it is.

CASSANDRA'S STORY

Six years ago I went to one of Sharon's workshops. I didn't really have any issues with my periods; I was just interested in how my cycle impacted my life. I am in my mid-30s and own a small marketing consultancy, and I wanted to see if this information would help me with my team and leadership skills. The workshop was a heap of fun and I left charts in hand and feeling really excited.

At first I just started to jot down words, and I wasn't really sure what I was doing. But I just stayed with it. I stayed in touch with Sharon and she gave me tips and reminders from the workshop on what to chart. I also noted everything she said in my chart each month. Slowly I built up my confidence in listening to my body.

Each day I would look at what day it was in my cycle. It would give me an idea of what to look for in strengths in my body and made me feel more connected to who I was as a woman. I really started to embrace all the different aspects of me, ones I never really connected to before.

Each night I would sit for just a few minutes and listen to my thoughts. I would close my eyes and feel what was going on in my body. I would even visualise the changes happening.

Years later I am now a pro at charting; I still chart regularly. Sure, I miss a few days and sometimes even a week or two, but when I feel a little shaky or my confidence begins to wane, I just get back to regular charting and within days I feel better.

I now use the charts to plan ahead. Each month I write up my chart and I include what is happening for me in the month ahead. I can see what phase I will be in at different events throughout the month and this allows me to support myself accordingly. So, for example, if I have a heap of events on around my Persephone phase, I make sure I schedule in time for me. I book a massage on the weekend and give myself some time off. Likewise, I make sure if I want to do some planning for the business, I give myself time in Daphne to do so. I just feel so powerful!

I joke with Sharon that she has unlocked a super power inside me, but some days that is exactly how I feel. I have always loved being a woman, and now I understand why. We have a pretty amazing gift with our menstrual cycle.

There are four further steps outlined below that will assist you to empower yourself to become an emgoddess: communicating, playing, planning and sharing.

You have explored the individual goddess energies from Chapter 2 and have seen some of the ways in which you express each of the phases in your cycle. You have discovered the tool of charting and the power it brings when you understand why you are feeling the way you do at different times of the month. Your task now is to develop this to the point where it becomes a beneficial tool in your everyday life.

Four further
steps to become an
emgoddess!

Start talking to your friends using the Emgoddess language. You could bring a cake into the office with the declaration 'I'm in Demeter today so I have done some baking!' The more you start to change the language around menstrual cycles, the more likely attitudes will change.

While speaking to others and creating the Emgoddess ripple effect, it is important to stay in touch with your inner thoughts and feelings. You will know this well through charting, but you can add another layer to this through meditation. This was a concept I had dabbled with on and off for many years. Remember that life-changing event I mentioned when talking about my move to stop drinking? On my retreat I connected with my inner goddess through meditation and it has changed my morning routine forever. I have tailored Emgoddess meditations I listen to at least once a week that help me to ground myself and really connect with the phase I'm in. There are always weeks where you will float through and become so tied up in the day to day you forget to meditate, but please don't tell yourself off; you are only human! Instead, get back on track as soon as you can so you can continue to enjoy beautiful space and time out that is just for you.

PLAYING

Start to identify the different phases and see how they are expressed for you; some women really connect with one particular phase. Do you align with one phase? I immediately think of particular friends when visualising the four individual goddesses. The other phases do exist within these women, but they are more subtle. Just because you are not a carbon copy of what I have described in this book does not mean you aren't experiencing the phases.

Charting will demonstrate this, revealing sometimes understated variations that may actually be more prominent than you realised. Some women really relate to Daphne and feel they are like this throughout the month, which I typically hear from clients who are career oriented: they're self-sufficient, determined to climb the corporate ladder and have little or no interest in children or what comes with mothering.

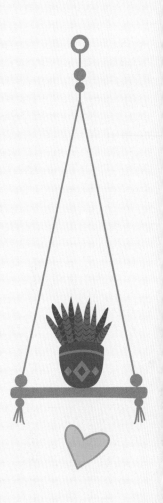

For most of the month Daphne women feel their energies very strongly. To experience the inward directions of Hecate in a strong Daphne type, I recommend meditation or yoga in the Hecate phase of the month.

Motherly Demeter can't help but be supportive and kind to others. Women who identify as Demeter are typically very practical and steady and also very popular: the person that friends always come to and rely on for advice, comfort and love. To experience Persephone for a Demeter-type woman, I recommend wearing lovely red silky underwear during the Persephone phase or putting colouring pencils to paper and drawing whatever comes to mind.

Persephone, really is a driven and passionate woman who would not wear pretty pastel colours if they were the last choice! For women who identify strongly with Persephone I urge them to experience and encourage their Daphne phase by ensuring all new ventures begin during Daphne; it's in Daphne that you join a gym or start doing yoga. I also recommend Persephone women to be a little more social during the Daphne phase.

A strong Hecate-influenced woman is inclined to be very spiritual and inward and would much rather be alone with a good book to read than surrounded by people. For such women I encourage the Demeter phase to be explored: spend more time with friends, go for a walk through the park or bake a cake for your colleagues at work.

You don't have to change your personality to experience the phases. You notice, encourage and enhance the subtle differences that make you the wonderful woman you are all month long.

SANDY'S STORY

As a natural therapist I have always believed that our menstrual cycles are a very important part of being a woman. I knew so many health conditions are impacted when cycles are out of alignment. I treated many women who had a range of menstrual-cycle conditions, so I was excited to hear more about Sharon's work.

Coming along to the workshop I prepared to hear all about how the changes in hormones throughout the month impacted moods and emotions and of course physical changes. But I was so intrigued in the changes in clothing and make-up — so much so I started to introduce this into my life and I love it!

I am a playful person at heart and like to mix things up a bit, so I love changing my dress sense depending on where I am in my cycle. It's like the days when I was younger and dressing up to be something different. But when I do this within my cycle I am just embodying the phase I am going through.

I wear my joggers and more sporty clothing when I am in Daphne; I pull out the natural lip gloss, pop on just a little bit of make-up and off I go. I deliberately look for more pretty colours: pastels and brights. My hair is quite long, so I love putting it up and wearing a ribbon or putting some clips in it.

When I move into Demeter I pull out my more floral and feminine lines; I love to wear a flowing dress or skirt. Most of my clothing is made from natural fibres, but I love really looking for linen or 100 per cent cotton as it makes me feel so connected to the earth. I love the feeling of my body in this phase, so I tend to wear underwear that supports me and makes my curves stand out. I feel like a true goddess!

Persephone is a funny phase for me: the early part is very sexy, my body is still feeling fantastic and everything I put on seems to feel fantastic. My work friends all laugh because they know what phase I am in as the leopard skin shoes often appear. I feel great.

However, towards the end of Persephone the drop is significant, so I really move into my black clothing and clothing that I know looks good on me no matter what phase I am in. This gives me more confidence; I'm more conservative and not putting myself out there so much. I feel more aware of my appearance and my moods, so I make sure I wear things that make me feel good inside.

Finally I am in Hecate, a phase of comfort and ease. I am menstruating, so it's important I feel comfortable. The elastic-waisted trousers and overshirts are sometimes the option, companioned with stylish but flat shoes. I like a more simple look here as I am focusing more on reconnecting to me.

This expression in my clothing keeps me connected to which phase I am in and how I can embrace the goddess energy to benefit me.

PLANNING

Now you have all this newfound knowledge and understanding about your monthly cycle and how it influences your mood and self-esteem, how can you harness it and look at the different phases positively? The trick is in planning: look at what events you have coming up and in which phase they will fall. How can you use this to your benefit? How can you support yourself better?

On day 1 of your cycle sit with your blank dial. Complete all the basics as you have done for the past few months, including the day of the week, the day in your cycle and the date and day of the month. Pop key dates coming up into your diary: maybe you have a large presentation, some key assignments due in your study or a significant birthday party coming up. Add in activities you know need to be completed; for example, you may have some work reviews that need to be completed or some planning ahead done. By putting in these dates you can see where it sits in your month; pencil in the phases based on your days.

Look at the four phases of the month and schedule events to suit. If you have a project you really need to get started schedule it for the Daphne phase. If you have meetings coming up with someone you need to win over for a deal, pop this into your Demeter phase. If you have to do some creative writing, schedule it for your Persephone phase. Maybe you have some review or reflection that needs to actioned? Put this into your Hecate phase. Doing this will allow you to match the strengths of your phase with the activities you need to do.

You can't schedule everything to suit perfectly. Maybe you have a large presentation that falls smack bang in Hecate, and you know from your charting that you may not feel your best at this time and may be low in energy. Knowing this beforehand will allow you to prepare better. If this is the case you can, for example, schedule extra time for a rest before the presentation so you can get your thoughts together. Maybe you can organise someone to assist you, either with parts of your workload or just for some moral support. You can adjust your diet, get some extra rest and ensure you are in the best place you can be at that phase of the month.

I like to write out some charts for the three upcoming months. My cycle may change very slightly in days so I can't write the exact dates, but I have an idea of the length of my cycle. I pop in activities I know are coming up and plan around them. Give it a try! This is where Emgoddess can really help you to transform your life.

SHARING

Share with others what you are discovering about yourself and enjoy all the wonderful aspects that make up you! When I first discovered Emgoddess I was managing a team of women. We were all very different, just as in every workplace; however, by using my knowledge of Emgoddess, I was able to support the team better. Knowing where others were in their cycle allowed us as a team to schedule who was working one on one with customers, who was doing more of the

creative work and who needed to have some space. It created a wonderful workplace in which we could communicate and support each other, as everyone was able to tap into their best as much as possible.

Describing the phases as different goddesses has created a different language for you to use. I am not advocating you avoid using medical terms as I think it's very important we do use the correct terms, but I am advocating some code language to soften situations. For example, when I am having a difficult day I don't like saying to my partner I am in the premenstrual phase of my cycle as it has a negative connotation — and, after all, the luteal phase is

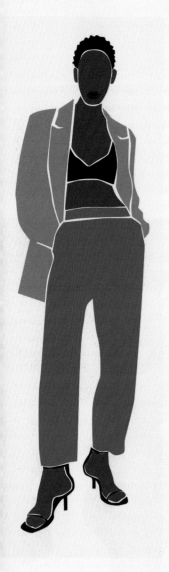

powerfully creative and will enable you to get through lists of tasks. Instead, explaining I am in Persephone is a more positive way of expressing myself. There are so many ways you can use the Empowerment Cycle to take your understanding of yourself to the next level.

The remainder of this chapter is dedicated to showing you some practical examples of how you can use the four phases to plan ahead and make the most of your newfound appreciation for your menstrual cycle.

UNICORN LEADERS

I have always been keen to find ways of using the Empowerment Cycle to become a better leader, so when I came across an article in *Forbes* in 2018[70] that listed the eight characteristics of a great leader, it piqued my interest:

- sincere enthusiasm
- integrity
- great communication skills
- loyalty
- decisiveness
- managerial competence
- empowerment
- charisma.

I have been fortunate enough to rub shoulders with many female leaders and *all* of them show *all* of these characteristics . . . but *not* at the same time! Unless you know someone you could dub a unicorn leader, or someone with all eight characteristics, I think you would be better off understanding your cycle and seeing how you can still be an awesome leader by tapping into each of these qualities at different times of the month.

Sheryl Sandberg's book *Lean In*[71] talks about the different leadership pressures between men and women in the workplace. She explains that when a man is assertive he is seen as being a powerful, strong leader with a 'take no prisoner' approach, a one-style only method to leadership that is accepted and respected by all around them, but when a woman shows the same approach to her leadership style she is seen as being a complete bitch.

I have witnessed female leaders working through this by facing the challenge, pushing back and allowing themselves to manage in whatever style suits them best. My own struggle is that I am  not that one style of management kind of girl: I have moments of strength, but sometimes I have a more understanding and softer approach – and it's not because I am feeling weak or disempowered by others around me! The truth is, many female managers intuitively lead differently depending where they are in their cycle and use the strengths that appear at different times of the month for them. Imagine what could happen if you were laser focused on your ability to know where you are in your cycle? Imagine as a leader understanding and utilising this tool, a tool we all have access to.

Women should embrace each phase and allow the strengths each phase brings – creativity, patience, inspiration or reflection – to shine through. I don't believe you need to be any one type of leader, as your gift is the diversity you embody through your cycle each and every day. Your body changes throughout the month, which impacts your ability and strengths. There are times of the month when you have a huge amount of energy, you are a clear communicator and have clear direction in your thoughts, and other times when you are more focused on empowering others and showing dedication and loyalty to those around you. You also have a time when your strengths are in your managerial ability and steadfastness to the task and times when you are more intuitive to the needs of your business and your people. This is not a coincidence: the biochemical changes that happen in your body each and every month influence all manner of changes in your management style. The

four phases highlighted throughout this book also impact the level of tolerance you may have for things and people, how creative you are in your thoughts and how passionate you are about getting something over the line.

Imagine, as a leader, understanding and utilising this tool. Below are some activities I recommend if you are in pursuit of unicorn leadership that will allow you to maximise the power given to you throughout your cycle.

Daphne, days 6 to 13: tap into the phase of power. In this more energetic and enthusiastic phase, you will lead by being very clear in your vision and enthusiasm. Embracing your goals, developing your plan and inspiring all around you, they can't help but be drawn to go along with you.

Demeter, days 14 to 17: make hay. This phase is a more compassionate stage and often allows you more time and patience, resulting in you being more encouraging. It is a great time to be supportive and ensure others are nurtured and achieving great things for all.

Persephone, days 18 to 28: dig in. This phase can be more challenging, as your emotions will be heightened and you will seem to put more demands on yourself and those around you. You can be more sensitive to the comments of others and may be a little more abrupt than usual. However, when you are aware and supported, this phase can bring great creativity to a project or challenge that has been in your sights.

Hecate, days 1 to 5: reflect on your work. This inward phase is strongly anchored in reflection and insight and allows you to assess and evaluate current situations with a sense of calmness and understanding.

If you are an athlete, you can become more aware of where you are in your cycle each time you train or compete, allowing you to take the appropriate physical and mental steps to ensure you are performing at your best.

Daphne, days 6 to 13: take it to the max. In this phase, athletes can achieve powerful training results and have the benefit of faster tissue repair time. If you are preparing for a major competition or event, now is the time to up the ante and slightly extend your training times. This will be the phase where you'll want to emphasis sprints or high-intensity interval training workouts. However, don't be completely fooled by your feelings of endless energy: you will need to be mindful that you need to incorporate time to recover so you don't overwork your body. If your competitions are being held during your Daphne phase, know that your body will be operating at its peak if you are taking care of your nourishment and levels of rest. Keep this in mind for an additional mental boost while you are doing your thing!

Demeter, days 14 to 17: the power of endurance. This phase is all about endurance; you have the ability to tap into sustained power and energy if you choose to. Demeter is thus a great phase for working on cardio and improving your long game. However, be mindful that knee joints can loosen during ovulation – a result of hormone shifts – which can make you vulnerable to anterior cruciate ligament injury. If this is a concern for you, try changing up your training regime to include lower-resistance methods for your legs. If you are competing while in Demeter, you can take precautions with your knees and add extra strapping if your sport relies heavily on your legs.

Focus on upper body training during this phase

Persephone, days 18 to 28: focus on the upper body. Training anything to do with your lower body may feel like an uphill battle during this phase, and motivation to exercise at all might be an issue. Understand that exercise can help to lower your stress levels and help with PMS symptoms if you are prone to experiencing them. Try focusing on arm curls and upper body training and keep lower body work on the lighter side. You will have better coordination during

this phase, so try leaning towards boxing, yoga, Pilates or a light aerobic session. You may feel more puffed than usual due to the increase in progesterone during this phase, but if you cannot avoid a high-intensity workout make sure you allow extra recovery time. Protein should be an important component of training nutrition in this phase, and getting some in during the 30-minute post-training window will help you to maximise your results.

Knowing your upper body is your secret weapon will be a great advantage if you are competing during this phase in a sport that favours upper body strength. However, if your sport is heavily geared towards the lower body, you need to give your legs a little more TLC.

Hecate, days 1 to 5: lower the tempo. Sport can feel harder during Hecate, but as an athlete you often don't get the choice to rest on your laurels. It sounds counter intuitive, but you will get the best lower body results at this time of the month and leg training will have the added benefit of offsetting your cramps. If you're someone who experiences dysphoria around menstruating, training during and especially right after menstruation might help to combat its effects by increasing a sense of control of your body and musculature.

If you are competing during the Hecate phase, be mindful you will need to give yourself extra TLC with nutritious foods and plenty of rest to be in good condition to perform. Ensure you also build in a longer recovery time so you don't deplete all of your reserves.

HOW RACHEL USES THE EMPOWERMENT CYCLE TO UP HER GAME IN THE SURF

I would describe myself as pretty competitive. I surf and I want to reach the highest level I can in my sport and I work really hard to do so. It's tough out there and we are always looking for ways to improve. After I finished training early one night I was told to go into the club to listen to a woman who was going to teach us about our menstrual cycles and training. I was dreading it. I don't like talking about my periods at the best of times, and now I had to sit with the girls I surf with and share details!

To my surprise, it was excellent. Sharon spoke about how our cycle is split into four phases, and if you want to, you can use your body more like a compass providing guidance on how to work with our strengths of the phase instead of against our bodies.

I was not aware of times when I was more prone to injury, when I had a better ability to take on instructions and when I needed to rest. I have been charting for the past six months and use this information to plan ahead. Each month I sit at my first day of my period and write out my chart. I mark up training and competitions and plan my training and eating around my cycle.

I know it's helping: I feel more in control of my training program and my body than ever before. I can understand days when I can kill it and days when I even sit out of some drills as I know they are not for me. It really is my secret weapon.

The life of a student is a busy one: keeping on top of homework assignments, exams and work and also having a social life. It's a lot to juggle, so charting will be a powerful tool to help you become more aware of how your moods, energy levels and zest for social interaction are affected by each phase.

Daphne, days 6 to 13: pump up the action. This is your phase! As your oestrogen is increasing, so is your ability to do more. You are in a great space to put in longer days, knock out assignments and really make hay while the sun shines. This phase is a great time to do all of your planning for the week and set your goals. You can achieve so much more in this phase, especially toward ovulation. The one thing to watch is that you do not push yourself too hard, as this is a time when you can overdo it. Make sure you balance your urge to conquer tasks and perform at your best with giving yourself time to go for a walk or run, hit the gym or yoga class and catch up with friends.

Demeter, days 14 to 17: the powerful communicator. If you can pick your time to present to a group this is it! This high-oestrogen phase brings with it the ability to communicate better. Your focus on listening will be heightened, and you will be more articulate and speak from the heart, meaning you will be able to clearly express yourself with compassion and thought. This is the perfect time to step up if there are any conflicts that need to be resolved with family members or friends, and you will be in a position to really be there to support your loved ones if they are going through a rough time.

This phase still has a level of high endurance so you can continue with some bigger days at work or studying, but achieving what you want is the main aim here. If you are working in a group you will be able to step into your power, bring people together and encourage them to follow your lead.

Persephone, days 18 to 28: an eye for detail. After ovulation you will still have a great few days when you can smash out some work, however, the sudden drop in oestrogen and temporary increase in progesterone can leave you less energetic. You might feel a bit tired and less inclined to get excited about seeing friends or hitting the town. This phase can test your patience with people and situations, so allow yourself some space. Be mindful that you may be more inclined to have knee-jerk reactions to things, so give yourself time to recharge and assess things before reacting throughout the phase. You will be much more focused on highly detailed tasks, even drawn to

them, and you will be partial to writing a checklist, a methodical process that is perfect for your inner Persephone.

Now is also the time to let your creativity flow. If you can give yourself time to play – dance, sing, draw, whatever it is for you – you will be able to channel this passion and feisty energy into something creative you can explore.

Hecate, days 1 to 5: reflect and recharge. Your period brings with it a drop in hormones and a drop in energy. Stay with it rather than fighting against it, and rest, sleep and relax. If you can, find time to look back over the month and see how you're tracking. Don't push yourself: if you have exams, ensure you have allowed enough time for sleep as a lack of sleep is not going to serve you well.

LETTING GO OF NEGATIVE THINGS

You have decided you want to give up something: it could be drinking, smoking, gambling or any other vice that has been holding you back. You know now it is no longer serving you and you are prepared to make a change and reclaim that part of yourself back.

Congratulations! You can adapt this plan to whatever it is you are choosing to release, although I've used alcohol as an example here.

Daphne, days 6 to 13: plan your attack. Sit down with your chart and diary and plan. Identify your support and your strategies for when you hit a bump in the road. Ensure you have everything you need: if you need to go shopping and get your stock of goodies, this is the time to do it. Grab a box of hot chocolate to have at night instead of a wine, or purchase soda water and fresh limes you can cut and put in as a refreshing drink alternative.

Plan out the month by highlighting danger times: when you may need to phone a friend, book in a massage or go to an extra gym class. If you have children or have spent any time around young ones, you will know that being worn out leaves little room for wasting energy on worrying, so wear yourself out! When we want to distract children we take them out to the park and let them run and run, so that by the time we get

home they are asleep in the car. It's the same theory here: if you are edgy, go for a run or book in an extra class. This phase brings high energy, and you need to put it to good use.

Demeter, days 14 to 17: buckle up. I'm going to be honest with you: Demeter is not the ideal phase to choose to give up something because the hormone shifts in your body make you more receptive to addiction. Therefore, if you already do enjoy a few too many wines of an evening, it will be harder to let it go. In fact, if you have been charting for a while before deciding to kick a habit, you may find your wine intake increases slightly during Demeter because your body tends to crave reward and you will seek out things that can fulfil that need.

When you choose to give up something harmful Demeter will dutifully roll around once a month, but by charting ahead you can highlight this phase and be better prepared. Planning ahead will allow you to see the few days when the desire may increase, and you

can put into place some alternative rewards. Think of something else you love such as a massage, indulgent dinner, luxe chocolate or whatever you need to keep you away from the wine fridge. Support yourself here; you need to be kind to yourself.

You need to be kind to yourself

Persephone, days 18 to 28: just avoid it! The happy hormones will be rapidly dropping and you may find you don't even feel like a drink as your cravings have lessened. If you do continue to partake in some beverages, you'll find the alcohol can exacerbate PMS symptoms and really make you feel awful. My advice is to just steer clear of it. If you slip up and notice how crappy you feel during this phase, it may be an encouragement to continuing on your path to sobriety. Chart honestly, so you remember how you felt the next time Persephone rolls around.

Remember, this phase loves a checklist, so you could design one you can tick off each day so you know you're on track and getting through your days.

Hecate, days 1 to 5: breathe. You are through the worst of your cravings and, with low hormones, the desire to get into a bottle of wine will often be reduced. Relax, make yourself a beautiful herbal tea and sleep.

CONCLUSION

The journey I embarked on to create Emgoddess and the empowerment cycle has been a long one, but one that has filled up my cup more than I could ever have anticipated. I quite like who I am; I truly do. It took a while for me to get to a stage in which I recognise and acknowledge all the different parts that add up to the whole me. It hasn't always been this way.

As a young person of 15 I remember playing hockey, my favourite sport, in the highest grade. I played the hardest and best I could, but if I had an off day and missed a few traps, gave away possession too easy or missed an easy tackle, I would spend the rest of the week pleading with my coach to drop me from the side. I would cry and become very dark. Alternatively, if I had a great game and rarely made a mistake I was full of life and happy. I was always trying to make others happy so they would like me.

Discovering in my early 20s the power of my menstrual cycle changed my life forever. I *love* who I am and am passionate about flicking on light switches for as many women as possible. If you have completed this book and feel more empowered and prepared to take on the world while loving the skin you are in, I am doing a happy dance! The four distinct phases women journey through each month impact everything about them: their energy levels, moods and emotions and physical health. Where we are in our cycle also impacts the

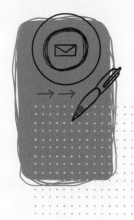

relationships we have with others, how we interact and our outward expression.

My journey initially helped me with my self-esteem, but it has now become much more than that. It has brought awareness to my physical and mental health and given me a powerful tool to use every day of my life. Emgoddess gives you the tools to track and identify where you are in your cycle and helps you to create ways to embrace and embody the energies of that phase, have a more positive relationship with your body and look at your cycle as the gift it really is.

For me and thousands of other women, Emgoddess is a way of life.

I am determined to do my part in providing other women with the tools to become more confident and self-assured individuals. From being a woman suffering from low self-esteem constantly, over time I have developed self-respect and self-love that continues to grow each day. I enjoy sitting quietly and journalling, and thinking deeply about how I truly feel inside. I also have positive qualities I continue to focus on. I am not perfect, and I love that too. For all the things that may not be strengths about me, I have many more attributes that shine out each and every day. I still have good and bad days, but when I feel a little lost I get back to my charting and almost instantly feel better about myself.

The Emgoddess model focuses on establishing global understanding that can bring joy to life and boost self-esteem for every woman. It touches women from all walks and stages of life, from young women who are just discovering their cycles to women who have been cycling for years with no real connection. I hope it can help you fall back in love . . . with you.

While this book gives you a comprehensive overview of everything I have learned and developed, you may find you need more personalised support. If this is you, please reach out to me through www.emgodess.com.au.

REFERENCES

1. Female Population of the World, Data World Bank, 9 November 2016, retrieved from http://data.worldbank.org/indicator/SP.POP.TOTL.FE.ZS?end=2015&start=1960.

2. Valerie Sirbert, 'Nearly half of women have experienced "period shaming"', *New York Post*, 3 January 2018, retrieved from http://nypost.com/2018/01/03/nearly-half-of-women-have-experienced-period-shaming.

3. Dr Nancy Etcoff and Dr Susan Paxton, Dove Global Beauty and Confidence Report 2016.

4. H. Golombeck et. al, 'Personality functioning status during early and middle adolescence', *Adolescent Psychiatry*, 1987, 14, 365-77.

5. Greg Jenner, 'How did women in the past deal with their periods? The History of Menstruation', retrieved from http://www.gregjenner.com/history-of-periods-and-tampons/, 29 December 2015; *A Million Years in a Day: A curious history of ordinary life from the Stone Age to phone age,* Thomas Dunne Books, 2016.

6. Maria Kaczmarek and Sylwia Trambacz-Oleszak, 'The association between menstrual cycle characteristics and perceived body image: a cross-sectional survey of Polish female adolescents', *Journal of Biosocial Science*, May 2016, 48(3): 374-90.

7. Rosalind Brock, Georgina Rowse and Pauline Slade, 'Relationships between paranoid thinking, self-esteem and the menstrual cycle', *Archives of Women's Mental Health*, April 2016, 19(2): 271-9.

8. Sarah E. Hill and Kristina M. Durante, 'Do women feel worse to look their best? Testing the relationship between self-esteem and fertility status across the menstrual cycle', *Personality Social Psychology Bulletin*, December 2009, 35(12): 1592-601.

9. Ingrid Johnston-Robledo et. al, 'Reproductive shame: self-objectification and young women's attitudes toward their reproductive functioning', *Women & Health Journal*, September 2008.

10. Deborah Schooler et. al, 'Cycle of shame: menstrual shame, body shame, and sexual decision-making', *Journal of Sex Research, November 2005, vol. 42, no. 4.*

11. *ibid.*

12. Johnston-Robledo et.al, *'Reproductive shame'*, February 2007, Women & Health 46(1):25-39.

13. Schooler et.al, 'Cycle of shame', J Sex Res, November 2005, 42(4):324-34.

14. Blanca Romero-Moraleda et. al, 'The influence of the menstrual cycle on muscle strength and power performance*', Journal of Human Kinetics*, August 2019, 68: 123-33.

15. Lisbet Wikström-Frisén, Carl-Johan Boraxbekk and Karin Henriksson-Larsen, 'Increasing training load without risking the female athlete triad: menstrual cycle based periodized training may be an answer?', *Journal of Sports Medicine and Physical Fitness*, November 2017, 57(11): 1519-25.

16. Leslie A. Consitt, Jennifer L. Copeland and Mark S. Tremblay, 'Endogenous anabolic hormone responses to endurance versus resistance exercise and training in women', *Sports Medicine*, 2002, 32(1), 1-22.

17. Erin Lyons, 'Sexism or science? AFLW investigates if players' periods linked to ACL injuries', *10 Daily*, 18 February 2020.

18. Birgitta Hellström and Ulla Maria Anderberg, 'Pain perception across the menstrual cycle: phases in women with chronic pain', *Perceptual and Motor Skills*, 11 February 2003, 96(1): 201-11.

19. Jennifer Chen, 'Women, are your hormones keeping you up at night?, Yale Medicine, 10 July 2017.

20. Nina R. W. Geiker et. al, 'A weight-loss program adapted to the menstrual cycle increases weight loss in healthy, overweight, premenopausal women: a 6-mo randomized controlled trial', American Society for Nutrition, July 2016, 104(1) :15-20.

21. Jeff Kiesner, 'Physical characteristics of the menstrual cycle and premenstrual depressive symptoms', *Psychological Science*, 2009, 20:763.

22. Laura Victoria Ortego-Leanoard and Irma Yolanda Del Rio Portilla, 'Creative thinking and its relation to the menstrual cycle', *Journal of Behavioral, Health & Social Issues*, 2012, 4(2): 91-102.

23. Concordia University, 'Map-reading more difficult for women during ovulation', *Science Daily*, 21 September 2016, retrieved from www.sciencedaily.com/releases/2016/09/160921115926.htm.

24. Stephanie C. Lazzaro et. al, 'The impact of menstrual cycle phase on economic choice and rationality', *PLOS One,* 29 January 2016, 11(1): e0144080.

25. University of California, 'Women's voices become more high-pitched during ovulation', *Science Daily,* 29 October 2008.

26. Hill and Durante, 'Do women feel worse to look their best?' *Personality and Social Psychology Bulletin*, September 2009, 35(12).

27. Seppo Kuukasjärvi et. al, 'Attractiveness of women's body odors over the menstrual cycle: the role of oral contraceptives and receiver sex', *Behavioral Ecology*, 1 July 2004, 15(4): 579–84.

28. Jeffrey C. Schank, 'Do human menstrual-cycle pheromones exist?', *Human Nature*, 1 December 2006, 17(4): 449–70.

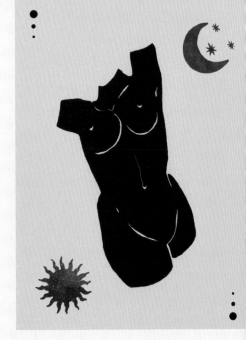

29. Claire Wilcox and Louann Brizendine, 'For women only: hormones may prevent addiction relapse', *Current Psychiatry*, vol. 5, no, 8, August 2006

30. R.R. Wetherill, T.R. Franklin and S.S. Allen, 'Ovarian hormones, menstrual cycle phase, and smoking: a review with recommendations for future studies', *Current Addiction Reports*, 1 March 2016, 3(1): 1-8.

31. Amy Lasek, 'Higher estrogen levels linked to increased alcohol sensitivity in brain's "reward center"', *Science Daily*, 7 November 2017.

32. Bertha J. Vandegrift et. al, 'Estradiol increases the sensitivity of ventral tegmental area dopamine neurons to dopamine and ethanol', *PLOS One*, 6 November 2017, 12(11): e0187698.

33. Suzette M. Evans and Frances R. Levin, 'Response to alcohol in women: role of the menstrual cycle and a family history of alcoholism', *Drug and Alcohol Dependence*, 1 March 2011, 114(1): 18-30.

34. United Nations Office on Drugs and Crime, *World Drug Report 2019.* 26 June 2019, retrieved from https://www.unodc.org/unodc/en/frontpage/2019/June/world-drug-report-2019_-35-million-people-worldwide-suffer-from-drug-use-disorders-while-only-1-in-7-people-receive-treatment.html.

35. Jill B, Becker and Ming Hu, 'Sex differences in drug abuse', *Frontiers in Neuroendocrinology*, 29 January 2008, (1), pp. 36-47.

36. Emily Anthes, 'She's hooked: allure of vices ties to a woman's monthly cycle', *Scientific American Mind*, 2010, 21: 14-15.

37. Laura Newcomber, 'Do women's periods really sync up?', retrieved from Greatist, https://greatist.com/health/womens-periods-sync#1, 10 February 2016.

38. Martha McClintock, 'Menstrual synchrony and suppression', *Nature*, 1971, (229), 244-5.

39. Frederick Naftolin et.al, *Menstrual Cycle Related Disorders Volume 7: Frontiers in Gynecological Endocrinology* (ISGE Series), Springer, 1st ed., 2 July 2019.

40. C.M. Lebrun, 'Effect of the different phases of the menstrual cycle and oral contraceptives on athletic performance', Sports Medicine Centre, University of British Columbia, Vancouver, Canada, 16 December 1993.

41. Romero-Moraleda et. al, 'The influence of the menstrual cycle on muscle strength and power performance', *Journal of Human Kinetics,* August 2019, 68: 123–133.

42. Brock, Rowse and Slade, 'Relationships between paranoid thinking, self-esteem and the menstrual cycle', *Arch Womens Ment Health,* April 2016,19(2):271-9.

43. Gregory A. Bryant and Martie G. Haselton, 'Vocal cues of ovulation in human females', *Biology Letters,* 23 Feb 2009, 5(1): 12-15.

44. Victor S. Johnstone et. al, 'Male facial attractiveness: evidence for hormone-mediated adaptive design', *Evolution and Human Behavior,* July 2001, 22: 251-67.

45. Paula Englander-Golden et. al, 'Female sexual arousal and the menstrual cycle', *Journal of Human Stress,* March 1980.

46. Kuukasjärvi et. al, 'Attractiveness of women's body odors over the menstrual cycle', *Behavioral Ecology,* July 2004, 15(4):579–584..

47. Brock, Rowse and Slade, 'Relationships between paranoid thinking, self-esteem and the menstrual cycle', *Arch Womens Ment Health,* April 2016,19(2):271-9.

48. Lasek, 'Higher estrogen levels linked to increased alcohol sensitivity in brain's "reward center"', 6 November 2017, retrieved from https://today.uic.edu/higher-estrogen-levels-linked-to-increased-alcohol-sensitivity-in-brains-reward-center.

49. Vandegrift et. al, 'Estradiol increases the sensitivity of ventral tegmental area dopamine neurons to dopamine and ethanol', 6 November 2017, retrieved from https://doi.org/10.1371/journal.pone.0187698.

50. Nicolas Guégen, 'Makeup and menstrual cycle: near ovulation, women use more cosmetics', *The Psychological Record,* 2012, 62: 3.

51. Alec T. Beall and Jessica L. Tracy, 'Women are more likely to wear red or pink at peak fertility', *Psychological Science,* September 2013, 24(9): 1837-41.

52. Paula Englander-Golden et. al, 'Female sexual arousal and the menstrual cycle', *Journal of Human Stress,* March 1980, 6(1): 42-8.

53. Mikako Sakamaki-Sunaga et. al, 'Effects of menstrual phase-dependent resistance training frequency on muscular hypertrophy and strength', *The Journal of Strength and Conditioning Research,* 1 November 2015, 30 (6).

54. Nina R.W. Geiker et. al, 'A weight-loss program adapted to the menstrual cycle increases weight loss in healthy, overweight, premenopausal women: a 6-mo randomized controlled trial', *The American Journal of Clinical Nutrition,* July 2016, 104(1): 15-20.

55. Brock, Rowse and Slade, 'Relationships between paranoid thinking, self-esteem and the menstrual cycle', *Arch Womens Ment Health,* April 2016,19(2):271-9.

56. Sarah E. Romans et. al, 'Mood and the menstrual cycle', *Psychotherapy and Psychosomatics*, 2013, 82(1): 53-60.

57. María del Mar Fernández et. al, 'Premenstrual syndrome and alcohol consumption: a systematic review and meta-analysis', *BMJ Open*, 2018, 8(3): e019490g.

58. Evans and Levin, 'Response to alcohol in women: role of the menstrual cycle and a family history of alcoholism', *Drug and Alcohol Dependence,* March 2011, 114(1):18-30..

59. E. Anne MacGregor, 'Menstrual migraine: therapeutic approaches', *Therapeutic Advances in Neurological Disorders*, 2009, 2(5), 327-36, doi: 10.1177/1756285609335537.

60. Leslie A. Consitt, Jennifer Copeland and Mark S. Tremblay, 'Endogenous anabolic hormone responses to endurance versus resistance exercise and training in women', *Sports Medicine*, 2002, 32(1), 1-22, doi:10.2165/00007256-200232010-00001.

61. Brock, Rowse and Slade, 'Relationships between paranoid thinking, self-esteem and the menstrual cycle', *Arch Womens Ment Health*, April 2016,19(2):271-9. .

62. Daphne M. Davis and Jeffrey A. Hayes, 'What are the benefits of mindfulness? A practice review of psychotherapy-related research', *Psychotherapy: Theory/Research/Practice Training*, June 2011, vol. 48, no. 2.

63. James N. Donald et. al, 'Daily stress and the benefits of mindfulness: examining the daily and longitudinal relations between present-moment awareness and stress responses', *Journal of Research in Personality*, 2016.

64. Brock, Rowse and Slade, 'Relationships between paranoid thinking, self-esteem and the menstrual cycle', *Arch Womens Ment Health*, April 2016,19(2):271-9. .

65. Sibylle Peterse and Tilman Eckloff, 'The role of the self-concept in the relationship of menstrual symptom attitudes and negative mood', Scientific Research, *Health*, 2011, vol. 3, no. 6, 326-32, DoI:10.423/health.2011.36056.

66. S. Alexander Haslam et. al, 'Social identity, health and well-being: an emerging agenda for applied psychology', *Applied Psychology: An International Review*, 2009, 58(1), 1-23.

67. Dr Xin Xu et. al, 'Characteristics of users of intrauterine devices and other reversible contraceptive methods in the United States', *Fertil Steril*, Guttmacher Institute, November 2011, 96(5):1138-44.

68. S. Abraham et. al, 'Menstruation, menstrual protection and menstrual cycle problems: the knowledge, attitudes and practices of young Australian women', *Medical Journal of Australia*, 1985, 142: 247-51.

69. Marni Sommer et. al, 'Neglect of menarche and menstruation in the USA', *The Lancet*, 2019, 393: 108188, 2302.

70. Kimberley Fries, '8 essential qualities that define great leadership', retrieved from https://www.forbes.com/sites/kimberlyfries/2018/02/08/8-essential-qualities-that-define-great-leadership/#103a756b3b63.

71. Sheryl Sandberg, *Lean In: Women, work, and the will to lead*, WH Allen, 2015.

ACKNOWLEDGEMENTS

I really want to thank all the people who have continued to support my work over the many years: I am so grateful for all their support as it is what has kept me on my pursuit to turn this worldwide taboo into an empowerment cycle.

To Roxy for helping me with finding the words for this book.

To my husband Rohan for all his support and love, and to my two beautiful children Indigo and Fox, who continue to make fun of me and my constant period talk.

ABOUT
THE AUTHOR

Sharon Wood is the founder and director of Emgoddess, which was established in 2015 and is a pioneering entity that is focused on changing perceptions and attitudes towards a topic not overtly discussed. She established Emgoddess in 2015, and it is now the vehicle through which she consolidates her own professional corporate journey and her passion to educate and empower others.

Sharon holds qualifications in holistic aromatherapy from the Tisserand Institute of London and meditation, along with multiple certifications in herbalism, natural fertility management and specialised aromatherapy.

She is driven to changing negative attitudes towards women's cycles by creating a way of looking at the cycle as a positive thing and is focused on establishing global understanding that can bring joy to life and boost the self-esteem of every woman. Her work touches women from all walks of life, from young women just discovering their cycles to women who have been cycling for years with no real connection.

For ever.

White blossoms had fallen from the trees.

They sprinkle white blossoms over the puppet of the
LITTLE BOY.

We all looked at each other
And tears ran down our cheeks.

SONG

For ever and for ever
Selfishness must pass
For ever and for ever
A friendship it will last.

GERAINT   And I remember saying
I'd really like you to have my bird
For ever.

KEITH   Thank you.

JULIA   And I said
I'd really like you to have my poem.
For ever.

GERAINT   Thank you.

KEITH   And I said
I'd really like us all to sing music.
For ever.

KEITH   It's a gift.

JULIA   A present.

GERAINT   A thank-you.

KEITH   To the Giant.

JULIA   The once Selfish Giant.

GERAINT   Who found kindness

KEITH   And shared it with us all

ALL   For ever.

JULIA   And as we were leaving the garden that day

KEITH   We saw a sign.

GERAINT   Not a Keep Out sign

JULIA   A new one.

KEITH   It said

They reveal the new sign.

ALL   For the children of the world.

SONG

Thank you, thank you, thank you
Our story we have told
Thank you, thank you, thank you
Your friendship is like gold

For ever and for ever
Remember selfishness must pass
For ever and for ever
A friendship true will last.

Thank you, thank you, thank you
Our story we have told
Thank you, thank you, thank you
Your friendship is like gold

END